T. M. PRUDDEN

ABOUT LOBSTERS

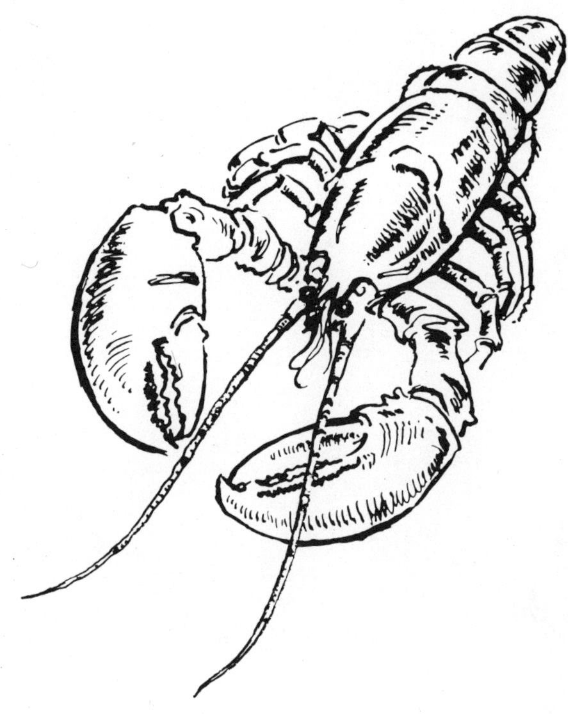

A JOHN MERRILL BOOK
THE BOND WHEELWRIGHT COMPANY
FREEPORT, MAINE

Third printing
Library of Congress Catalog Card Number: 62-21299
ISBN 0-87027-127-X
Manufactured in the United States of America

FOREWORD

There have been many articles written about the American lobster, but two such works stand out as being particularly authoritative and comprehensive. One is a section of the book *The Fisheries and Fishing Industries of the United States,* compiled by George Brown Goode, Assistant Director of the United States National Museum. It was published in 1884 by the U. S. Commission of Fisheries.

The second book, *The Natural History of the American Lobster,* by Dr. Francis Hobart Herrick, was published in 1895 as a bulletin of the U. S. Commission of Fisheries.

Both of these books are excellent in their detail and accuracy, but even Dr. Herrick's book is more than sixty-five years old. They deal largely with the biology and anatomy of lobsters, and are scholarly works in scientific language.

But in sixty-five years the increasing demand for lobsters has resulted in renewed researching of lobster habits, and some improvements in the methods of catching. This work intends to supplement, and bring up to date, Dr. Herrick's fine book. It is written for the use of those interested in the lobster industry, and is shorn of scientific language.

Notice how often it has been necessary to use the words "probably" or "it is believed." This indefiniteness is necessary because our knowledge of lobsters is far from complete.

ACKNOWLEDGMENTS

This work is indebted to the knowledge of many men. It is, in part, a compilation of information furnished by those who are foremost in their own trades.

Space does not permit listing all of them, but I am particularly indebted to:

Dr. Herrick and his *Natural History of the American Lobster*
Maine Department of Sea and Shore Fisheries
Dr. H. J. Thomas of the Scottish Marine Laboratory
Maine Coast Fisherman
Physiological Laboratory, Charlottenlund, Denmark
Maine Agricultural Experiment Station
William Benson, Portland, Maine
Harry Georgeopoulous, East Coast Lobster Pound
J. H. Patteson, Consolidated Lobster Company
Albert E. Brooks, Brooks-Sprague Corporation
Edward Myers, Saltwater Farm
John Hughes, Massachusetts Division of Marine Fisheries, Oak Bluffs, Mass.
U. S. Fish & Wildlife Service
William C. Shroeder, Woods Hole Oceanographic Institution
Ernest W. Barnes, Massachusetts Division of Fisheries & Game
Harold Look, Jr., Rockland, Maine

I am indebted to Robert Dow and Phillip Goggins of Maine Department of Sea and Shore Fisheries, who have reviewed this work, advised on its material, and corrected errors of fact.

T. M. Prudden

Hingham, Mass.
1962

PUBLISHER'S PREFACE TO THE 1973 EDITION

Much more has been learned about the lobster itself since this book was first published in 1962. According to Robert L. Dow, Director of Marine Research for the State of Maine since 1953, "In the last decade lobster research has probably increased our knowledge by a magnitude of ten or more."

According to figures supplied by the Maine Department of Sea and Shore Fisheries, 22,075,268 pounds of lobsters were landed in 1962 in 767,000 traps set by 5,658 registered Maine lobstermen, who were paid an average of .507 per pound. In 1972, the landings were only 16,256,458 pounds, though an estimated 1,247,000 traps were set by 7,045 registered Maine lobstermen. They were paid an average of $1.14 per pound. (Today prices are higher.) Thus in ten years landings have declined by nearly six million in spite of the fact that five million more traps were set by nearly two thousand more lobstermen than before.

The figures indicate that Prudden's call for continued research and improvement in the industry are even more valid than they were ten years ago. They also indicate a need for radical changes in management.

Departmental researchers in Maine have found that climatic cycles have influenced the abundance of inshore lobster populations throughout the range, New York to Newfoundland, and also the offshore populations south of New York.

Other factors may be even more important. The size at maturity of both male and female lobsters has been determined by Jay S. Krouse in a Lobster Research Program initiated in 1966 by the Maine Department of Sea and Shore Fisheries in cooperation with the U. S. Department of Commerce, National Marine Fisheries Service. Only a few females between 81- to 90-mm carapace lengths were found to be mature. At about 105-mm nearly all females were mature. From this it would seem evident that the minimum size law in Maine (81-mm carapace length) and elsewhere is, as Dow puts it "substantially too small to permit more than token numbers of females to reproduce once before they are caught."

Among other things such as product diversification as a means of better income for the lobsterman, Prudden advocated a better lobster pot that would "get away from wood and its buoyancy and its attraction to borers." Today there is a trend toward metal pots. According to Harold Arndt, a biologist and president of Marcrafts, Inc., of Freeport, Maine, who designed the aluminized welded wire mesh and vinyl-coated wire mesh traps they manufacture, between 200 and 300 were sold in 1967, over 10,000 in 1972; and the prediction is for over 15,000 nationally in 1973, judging by the number already sold. This is small compared to more than a million traps set in Maine alone, but the percentage of increase is impressive. These traps keep their full weight and are much more likely to hold their ground than wooden traps, and they are of course impervious to worms. They probably increase the efficiency of lobster trapping.

But according to Dow improvement in lobster pot design is not the answer, for traps themselves are a major source of the 28 to 36% annual mortality rate in lobsters "between the immediate sublegal class and the time the survivors reach legal size." One and a quarter to 2¾ million lobsters "are cannibalized or retained indefinitely in cut-off lobster traps." Others are killed by finfish on their way down to the bottom after being discarded by lobstermen.

Perhaps one answer as far as inshore lobster populations are concerned, is to be found through sea-farming, which Prudden also advocated. Today the culture of lobsters has gone beyond the experimental stage of the 1960's; it is apparently here to stay. Interested readers may learn about this through Dr. Donald Horton at TRIGOM, the Research Institute of the Gulf of Maine, 76 Falmouth Street, Portland 04103, of which the University of Maine is a member, that serves as a clearing house for information. At Martha's Vineyard, Massachusetts, at the hatchery run by the Department of Natural Resources, John Hughes reports on progress in sea farming. A man-constructed natural rock reef has been in operation in Canada for more than ten years, according to Mr. Dow, and the Department of Sea and Shore Fisheries of Maine has had a related structure since 1966, designed to attract lobsters to particular areas where they may be harvested easily. Rocky habitats are also being attempted by the Marine Experiment Station at the University of Rhode Island, Kingston.

All in all, the future may have to bring about a radical change in the lobster industry, in order for it to flourish, let alone survive. "We know with reasonable accuracy," Dow writes, "the size of the legal lobster populations in Maine and have been acceptably accurate in forecasting what the catch will be. We are reasonably certain that the legal supply could be increased approximately 40% by biologically sound management and elimination of trap associated mortalities. . . . I personally would recommend a complete about-face in the methods used for catching lobsters."

Over and over again in this book Prudden pointed out the advantages of education and open-mindedness on the part of lobstermen.

If he were alive today, he would no doubt urge every lobsterman to face the facts that are being elicited by vigorous research and to put every effort, even if it meant a slight sacrifice of individual independence, toward cooperation in making the industry ride creatively with those facts.

CONTENTS

LIST OF ILLUSTRATIONS

LIST OF TABLES

NOTE THESE TWO STARS: ★ ★

These stars mark parts of this work which are based on observations by lobstermen and others. Their opinions have been carefully culled to include only statements believed to be true.

But such observations are not scientifically proven facts.

PORTRAIT OF A LOBSTERMAN

Most problems in lobstering have to do with people. Hence, this picture of a lobsterman is placed at the beginning of this book.

Lobstermen are often a breed apart, as anyone might be who worked alone most of the day with only the expanse of the sea and his own thoughts to keep him company. The interest of his job lies in the repeated anticipation of what catch will be in the next pot he hauls; and if it is empty, hope and interest are revived for the succeeding haul. It is a lonely job, requiring getting up before dawn, and can be cold and wet and discouraging. The result is a distinctive personality, as described by a salesman of lobster plugs.

> Two brothers, young fellers, maybe thirty years old, run a well-found marine store. It is well up on the ledge and is reached by a sandy, two-rut road that seems to lead nowhere. But it does arrive at the shorefront in a clearing with several summer cottages, many of them overhanging the rocks.
>
> The two brothers are interested in plugs; they are courteous and on their toes. They think the plugs are good, but they want "Hen-ray's" opinion (Hen-ray being mentioned with deference as though he were the last word in lobstering).
>
> Fine. The three of them will go and tell the story to Hen-ray. They troop down a gravelly path, zig-zagging through the blueberry bushes and ending in a gangway spanning the water to a float.
>
> Hen-ray's vessel is the only one tied up, and is a fine craft—a 36-footer with a high stem, a handsome sheer and a square transom, painted white. Her port side is scarred, in spite of the horizontal strips of wood to protect against the banging of lobster pots. A cockpit takes up three-quarters of her length, and at present

holds two stinking baskets of bait, and several lobster pots standing on end.

And Hen-ray.

It is Hen-ray who dominates the picture. He isn't tall, perhaps five and a half feet, and he isn't young—he might be fifty, but his two-day growth of grey stubble may add to his age. He wears faded dungarees tucked into knee-length rubber boots, a gaudy flannel shirt, and a long-visored Portegee fisherman's cap. He chews tobacco slowly and monotonously.

Hen-ray has a strong face, seamed and tanned, and piercing blue eyes which impel one to look back with equal concentration. He is not the smiling type, and gravely greets the two brothers with "Mornin', boys."

The brothers make the introduction, and the salesman tells the story of the plugs. Hen-ray listens impassively, not quite antagonistic, but rather holding himself coldly aloof from this city slicker in store clothing who is brash enough to tell *him* about plugging lobsters. The sales talk ends with "Here's a handful. You try 'em."

There is no response in Hen-ray's face as he receives the plugs in a big knuckled hand. He doesn't even look at them, but continues to coldly and silently appraise this stranger. His jaws chomp on and the tension grows. Then he does examine the pile of plugs. He doesn't take one up singly to test its sharp point or scrutinize its shape. He is deliberate, and one can feel his unspoken contempt for them. Finally, he tosses the handful over his shoulder into the water, leans to the rail to spit overside, and says "Them plugs ain't wuth a good Goddam." He looks up with an icy glare to show that he isn't to be taken in by any lubber who doesn't know lobstering.

Of course, the salesman is angry. And he's also aware that Hen-ray expects him to be angry. The city feller swallows a couple of times to absorb the shock, and keeps glaring back just as piercingly as Hen-ray is looking at him. He takes out another handful of plugs, slowly and deliberately, and holds them out to Hen-ray. He tries to grin as he says, " Maybe so, Captain, but suppose you really examine these before you heave them overside."

Hen-ray receives the plugs, never taking his eyes away from the stranger, and just a twinkle replaces their frigid antagonism. It is enough to make his whole face light up. He spits again, and sits down on the wash-rail to examine the plugs with the sure movements of an expert.

When he looks up again he addresses the brothers: " Don't look so bad. I'll try 'em."

This is a portrait of one lobsterman.

I

Nature of Lobsters

Lobsters are scavengers. They are also cannibals.

They are essentially a bottom-living animal, using their powers of swimming only in an emergency. Caught lobsters seem sluggish, but in their natural element lobsters are agile, wary, pugnacious, capable of defending themselves against larger enemies, and on occasion and for short distances they exhibit surprising speed. Where several lobsters of equal size are kept in a tank they will usually live in peace. But if one is injured, as by the loss of a claw, it will be quickly attacked by the stronger and destroyed. This trait is one reason for plugging a lobster's claw.

Like all scavengers, they have highly developed senses for locating their food.[1]

Lobsters are essentially creatures of twilight, and explore the bottom in search of food mainly after sundown or at night, when it is usually more active than in daylight. Lobstermen know this, and it is the reason they leave pots down overnight.[2]

The lobsters of England, Scotland, and northern Europe are true lobsters in that they have crusher claws, as distinguished from crawfish and the so-called African " lobsters." They differ from the American lobster only slightly, chiefly in the rostrum or beak, which is narrower in the European lobster and has teeth only on its upper margin. European lobsters are usually smaller than the American.

Lobsters were in unbelievable abundance in the early days. Those thrown up on the beaches were a nuisance, and were used for fertilizer. A Hingham historian reports windrows of lobsters eighteen inches deep cast up after a hard storm. In early Plymouth days any youngster could wade out and capture by hand all he needed. An early re-

---

[1] *See* Taste, page 18.

[2] *See* Sight, page 17.

port records that lobsters five and six feet long were caught in New York Bay.

History

Lobster fishing as a separate industry seems to date from late 1700, and was first developed on the coast of Massachusetts, particularly Cape Cod. Some lobstering was done among the Elizabeth Islands and along the coast of Connecticut as early as 1810. Strangely enough, this industry was not extended to the coast of Maine until 1840.

In a pamphlet by Robert L. Dow, " The Story of the Maine Lobster," published by Maine Sea and Shore Fisheries, it says:

> The economic possibilities of the Maine lobster fishery were realized by nearly all pre-colonial explorers from England and Europe, even if almost two and one-half centuries were to elapse before a real lobster industry was established.
>
> Among the specific references to the lobster resource of the Maine coast is that contained in Rosier's account of Waymouth's voyage to Maine in 1605. Rosier said, " And towards night we drew with a small net of twenty fathoms very nigh the shore; we got about thirty very good and great lobsters . . . . which I omit not to report, because it sheweth how great a profit the fishing would be . . . . "
>
> That the Maine lobster was appreciated by the colonists is substantiated by the many references to their dependence upon the crustaceans for much of their food. However, the actual commercial development of the fishery did not take place until many years later.
>
> Just when Maine lobsters were first marketed is not entirely clear but the commercial importance of the fishery in supplying out-of-state markets did not come about until after 1840. Records of this period show that the lobster supply near the large market areas of eastern Massachusetts had declined appreci-

ably from the beginning of the nineteenth century. Observers believed that this decline in Massachusetts production was due to increased fishing intensity, lack of conservation, and a greater demand for the product.

It was during the decade 1840 to 1850 that Massachusetts dealers began looking to the Maine lobster grounds for a continuing supply of the species. Although some lobster fishing was done by local fishermen, even on a commercial scale, a large part of the annual catch was taken by Massachusetts boats operating in Maine waters.

Incidents comparable to the experience of one Captain Church and his smack *Monticello* in New Harbor are characteristic of the early development of the lobster industry in Maine. Church and his crew sailed into New Harbor in 1853 and began lobster fishing. Using hoop-net pots, Church's fishing operations were so intensive and his catch so large that the citizens of New Harbor threatened to drive him out of the harbor unless he ceased " catching up all the lobsters."

Production of lobsters on a commercial scale is believed to have been started in Western Maine waters about 1840. Gradually the fishery extended eastward, to Penobscot Bay by the late 1840's and to Eastport by 1855. It would appear that the bulk of the fishing was carried on by non-resident fishermen.

A demand for the fresh product in the large marketing areas of New York and Boston induced both resident and non-resident fishermen to specialize in the catching of lobsters; however, the history of the Maine canning industry indicates that the processing of lobster meat in hermetically sealed containers did more to stimulate the widespread exploitation of the resource than did the fresh market.

It is noteworthy that " the introduction of the lobster canning process at Eastport . . . . dates the beginning of the extensive canning interests of the United States in all its branches."

Employing canning methods obtained from France by way of Scotland and Nova Scotia, experiments in packing lobster meat were commenced in Eastport about 1840. By 1843 techniques had been so improved that the product was considered to be marketable. Although lobsters for the Eastport cannery during the early years had to be brought by smack from the western part of the state, the success of the new venture led, within the next thirty-five years, to the construction of twenty-three factories scattered along the coast as far west as Portland.

The spreading fame of Maine lobsters and the lack of adequate facilities for proper distribution of the fresh product were the two factors which stimulated the canning industry. As early as 1854 large quantities of Maine canned lobster were being shipped to California and to foreign markets.

An interesting sidelight on the canned lobster industry is that in 1879 a Southwest Harbor firm was canning whole lobster in the shell for the export trade. These lobsters were intended primarily for garnishing dishes.

Unfortunately, commercial catch data were not compiled prior to 1880 and even for some years thereafter but incompletely. According to estimates made in 1880 when nearly nine and one-half million pounds of lobsters were used to produce two million pounds of the canned product, the peak of canned lobster production came in 1870, and was followed by a decade of annual decline.

Restrictions affecting the canning of lobsters were first passed by the Maine legislature in 1872. From that time on the commercial importance of this phase of the lobster industry rapidly decreased. Subsequent legislation culminated in the so-called 10½-inch lobster law of 1895, a measure which put an abrupt end to an industry which had maintained itself by carefully avoiding even the most elementary conservation practices.

The commissioner of Sea and Shore Fisheries said of this law in 1904, "The (lobster) canning business, which received the blow given by the legislature of 1895 when it repealed the nine-inch law died in that year, and with the death of the canning industry the lobster business of the state commenced to revive."

Overdue as had been the end of the Maine canned lobster industry by 1895, this industry, nevertheless, had served several useful purposes. It had brought about the first exploitation, on a broad commercial basis, of the Maine lobster resource. It served to diversify fishing activities and to broaden the economy of coastal areas. It stimulated competition from the fresh lobster industry and forced the latter to improve handling, transportation and distribution methods and facilities. In a negative way, the canning industry had made obvious the need for conservation, law enforcement, and the elimination of prodigal waste in the fishery.

Following the final elimination of canning as an industrial factor, the fresh lobster industry took over the commercialization of the fishery in its entirety. Although it is uncertain when tidal pounds and other holding devices were first introduced into Maine waters, by 1904 twenty-six had been built with a total storage capacity of one and one-half million lobsters. Storage facilities currently employed for the holding of lobsters consist of some forty tidal pounds and approximately one thousand tanks and cars. It is possible to store nearly five million pounds of lobsters in these various holding devices.

To the fresh market area, within the limitations imposed on the live product by transportation and distribution facilities, holding devices provide much the same marketing service today as did the canneries to the canned foods market years ago. Live storage pounds have made possible the development and maintenance of more stable marketing conditions.

Sources of Lobsters[3]

There are two sources of lobsters consumed in the United States: domestic and Canadian. Practically all the U. S. lobsters are consumed in this country. Exports to Europe and Canada are negligible. Canadian lobsters are imported in response to the strong U. S. demand. About 65 to 80 per cent of the Canadian catch is exported to the U. S. This Canadian supply is an important factor in our lobster industry. Over 22 million pounds of live lobsters and frozen lobster meat and 2 million pounds of canned meat were imported in 1957. Maine catches were 24 million pounds. Actually, Canada's contribution to the U. S. consumer of lobsters is greater than these statistics indicate. First, the U. S. catch represents the lobsters caught, not the lobsters sold to large dealers, because mortalities occur during handling and holding operations. The Canadian imports represent lobsters which have survived these initial mortalities. Second, some of the Canadian imports are frozen lobster meat which requires about four pounds of live lobster for one pound of meat.

Both U. S. and Canadian lobster production have increased during recent years. For example, in 1938-1947, the average U. S. catch was 12 million pounds, and in 1948-1957, 21 million pounds. The corresponding Canadian catches were 34 and 47 million pounds.

In general, the lobster industry is in a fairly good economic condition compared to the years prior to World War II. It is not a source of great profit on either primary or secondary level, but it does provide a living for many people. As long as the industry shows no driving ambition to increase profits by modern methods of fishing, handling, and

---

[3] Information herein is taken from Leslie Scattergood and Robert L. Dow, "The Lobster Industry" (18th Report), presented at the 26th Meeting, North Atlantic Section, Atlantic States Marine Fisheries Commission (September, 1930).

processing, we can anticipate that fishermen will not ask for assistance.

Fresh Water

Lobsters will not live in fresh or brackish water, although it is debatable as to whether a slight admixture of fresh water is harmful to them or not. They are caught at the mouths of large rivers—as at Westport Island, Maine, where the water is decidedly brackish on top, but when placed in surface cars in the same locality they are said to perish quickly, indicating that the water must be much more salty at the bottom.

Lobsters affected by fresh water, particularly in tanks, will be swollen and puffy at the junction of the tail and solid shell. This swelling is so typical that the lobster dealer can usually diagnose the cause.

Habitat

The ranges of a lobster in depth are from low water to 225 fathoms. At such a depth the fishing with pots is uneconomical, the cost of so much warp is too great an investment, and the hauling of this much line takes too long. Twenty fathoms is the usual fishing depth.

Lobsters prefer a rocky bottom but flourish on gravel or sand bottom, especially those partially covered with the larger seaweeds such as kelp. This vegetation is not essential, for in times past they were notoriously plentiful on the bare sands off Provincetown. The kelp is probably attractive in shading the lobsters and hiding them from enemies. Lobsters apparently will live on any hard bottom where they can find food. Mud bottom is rarely attractive except in winter when some lobsters will burrow into mud, and when caught have mud adhering to their shells.

Bleeding and " Thrown " Claws

Bleeding of a lobster can be caused by a lost claw or a " thrown " claw. Soon after a claw is " thrown," the stump is covered with a crust of coagulated blood which prevents further bleeding until a skin is formed. When a claw plug is lost, however, the lobster does not so readily cease to bleed, probably due to internal injury to the flesh of the claw caused by the insertion of the plug. Thus a lost plug is very likely to cause the death of the lobster unless it is kept in sea water. A few lobstermen recognize this frailty and keep half a barrel of circulating sea water in the cockpit. The plugged lobsters are dropped into this barrel and are protected by the salt water from bleeding until a clot has formed.

The " throwing " of a claw does not occur between *any* of the joints but always at one particular point, near the upper end of the second or double joint, where it is smallest and encircled by a distinct groove. The claw cannot be broken off at this or any other place by main force without injury to the lobster, yet the lobster is able to " throw " its claw without any fuss or warning.

It is a common belief of lobstermen that a lobster ★ ★ which has lost a claw or been seriously maimed in any way will not shed until the injury has been repaired. One lobsterman, whose statements are respected, reports that bleeding can be stopped and the wound " cauterized " by applying ice, and that the shell of a soft lobster can be temporarily hardened by ice.

Migration

Most lobstermen agree that lobsters move offshore in cold weather and are sluggish and not eager for food. It is a fact hard to prove. It may be that lobsters have an instinct to protect themselves from the deep waves of winter storms, and that this instinct is triggered by the approach of cold weather. Thus any seaward migration might be in search of deeper, safer water rather than for warmer water. A plausible argument can be presented that lobsters hibernate somewhat like bears, and hardly move at all. The certain fact is that they are little attracted by bait in winter.

Lobstermen believe that in winter it takes hours ★ ★ for a lobster to sluggishly drag himself even a few feet to seek his food. Hence, the hauling of a pot daily in cold winter—even if the weather permitted—with the consequent scaring of a lobster which has started to crawl to the pot, does not bring good results.

Even in summer, some excellent lobstermen prefer a two-day set if they want to catch big ones. Their theory is that large lobsters are always sluggish and take hours to crawl to a pot. Thus it would seem that the best fishing would be through having twice as many pots as can be hauled in one day but only haul half of them each day.

If lobster migrations along the coast at any season were of considerable amount, it is evident that regions once depleted—as Provincetown—would be restocked by accessions from neighboring parts. Apparently this does not occur, and it seems as though each section of the coast is inhabited by a colony which tends to stay on its home grounds, so that if its numbers be once seriously depleted, its recovery will be slow.

A scientific study of lobster migration by Dr. D. G. Wilder of the Fisheries Research Board of Canada is reported in detail in *Maine Coast Fisherman* of June 1957. It says in part:

> Knowledge of lobster movements is so basic to sound management that the subject has received a great deal of attention in Canada, the United States and northern Europe.
>
> In Canada, lobster tagging has been carried on for over twenty-five years. Only lobsters in good condition were tagged, and the size and sex of each was recorded. The lobsters were liberated up to ten miles offshore at many different points around the coast.
>
> Over 100,000 lobsters have been tagged and over half of these have been recaptured by fishermen. Of one particular lot of 25,025, 16,696 were recaptured.

None of these had moved from one area to the other—a distance of about ten miles.

These tagging results, which are in general agreement with those reported from other countries, show that lobsters are not truly migratory. The great majority of tagged lobsters which have been recaptured were caught very close to the place where they were liberated. The few that do move appreciable distances seem to do so in a more or less random manner. Of more than 50,000 tagged lobsters, only three moved as much as sixty miles. It appears, therefore, that the lobster population is made up of a series of separate, independent stocks with very little mixing between areas. This conclusion is confirmed by the striking differences in the color, shape, sizes and sex ratios of lobsters from different areas. Rather marked differences have been observed in stocks separated by only a few miles. There is no evidence in the tagging results to suggest that lobsters make seasonal migration on and off shore. It is possible that in certain areas lobsters leave the immediate shore line and move into somewhat deeper water as winter approaches, but the tagged lobsters gave no indication of such behaviour.

In a later article, Dr. Wilder and R. C. Murray write:

It seems evident from our taggings that offshore and onshore movements have no appreciable effect on the catch of lobsters. How then do fishermen get the impression that such movements occur? Actual changes in the abundance and activity provide a logical explanation.

In the fall of the year the shallow inshore waters are relatively warm, the deeper offshore waters, considerably cooler. When the season opens, lobsters are plentiful and trap readily in the warm inshore waters. Intensive fishing soon reduces the inshore stocks, the shallow water cools rapidly, and the remaining lobsters become less active and harder to catch. As a result, the inshore catch falls off rapidly. At this stage the offshore stocks have not been fished hard, and the deeper water has not yet cooled a great deal. Consequently, the best fishing at this time is found offshore. Gradually, however, as the offshore stocks are reduced by fishing, and the deeper water cools, the catches drop off. In the spring, the inshore waters warm up quickly and the lobsters which escaped the fall fishery again become active and provide fairly good fishing. This pattern of fishing gives the false impression that the lobsters move offshore and onshore.[4]

Similar tagging and tests have been run by the Department of Natural Resources of Massachusetts, and by Maine's Department of Sea and Shore Fisheries. The number of tagged lobsters in each case was only a fraction of the number tagged by Canada, but the conclusions were the same, i.e., that lobsters cannot be considered migratory.

In the course of these tests there have been outstanding contradictions, such as the lobster tagged in Wareham and caught in Boston, presumably having passed through the Cape Cod canal, a journey of one hundred and thirteen days; or an oversized lobster tagged in Penobscot Bay and retrieved on the north shore of Massachusetts. These exceptions do not affect the overall picture; their number is too small, and it is probable that there are unusually vigorous and venturesome specimens among lobsters just as there are among all animals.

It has been suggested that limited migration might apply to smaller lobsters but not necessarily to the bigger ones.

Water Temperature vs. Catch

There is some difference in opinion between scientists to account for the fluctuations of the lobster catch in different seasons of the year. Robert L. Dow has published a nine-year record of lobster landings in July and August in

[4] *Maine Coast Fisherman* (September, 1958).

relation to water temperatures in the earlier spring months. He also shows the price fluctuations during this period.

Year	a *April-May Water Temp. Degrees F.*	b *July-Aug. post-moult lobster landings in millions of lbs.*	c *July-Aug. aver. landed price per lb. in cents*	d *Lobster landings in millions of pounds January-June following*
1952	47.6	7.1	42	4.1
1953	50.0	8.1	33	3.6
1954	48.5	8.1	34	3.8
1955	48.6	8.3	32	3.2
1956	45.0	5.1	50	4.1
1957	48.0	7.8	35	4.4
1958	45.8	6.0	50	4.4
1959	44.8	5.3	51	4.5
1960	46.6	6.5	44	4.3*
1961				4.27*

* Estimated

These figures show that the catch in July-August is greater when the sea water is warmer during the preceding April to May, but the landings fall off in the succeeding January to June. Notice how uniform the total catch is for each January to July except when warm spring water causes a greater catch in July to August. These figures permit a reasonable estimate of what the catch will be in midsummer if the spring water temperatures are known.

Increase in Fishing Effort

The number of traps in operation is a good indication of how hard lobsters are fished, and the records of their number are more consistent, and include a longer period of years, than any other factor likely to influence the magnitude of landings.

Thus the following figures are important.[5]

[5] Taken from Robert L. Dow, "The Role of Traps in the Maine Lobster Fishery."

Year	*Number of Traps in Thousands*	*Landings in Millions of pounds*
1940	222	7.6
1941	194	8.9
1942	187	8.4
1943	209	11.5
1944	252	14.1
1945	378	19.1
1946	473	18.8
1947	516	18.3
1948	459	15.9
1949	462	19.3
1950	430	18.4
1951	383	20.8
1952	417	20.0
1953	440	22.3
1954	488	21.7
1955	532	22.7
1956	533	20.6
1957	565	24.4
1958	609	21.3
1959	717	22.3
1960	745	24.0 (estimated)

The Senses

Sight. The eye of a lobster is a compound eye, as is that of the common house fly, and consists of perhaps 10,000 facets or little eyes. Sight is the lobster's poorest sense, and is probably almost nil in bright light. In fact, the greater part of its life is spent at depths where clear vision is impossible from lack of light, which indicates that sight ought to play but a small part in its daily life.

It has been suggested that some of the multiple ★ ★ eyes might be tremendously sensitive to light on a scale beyond our human comprehension. This is similar to the phenomenal acuteness of a hawk's eye, which is said to be able to sight a rabbit when the hawk is a mile high in the sky. If this were so, a lobster might be able to see much more clearly in the dimness of the ocean than was believed possible. The idea of different eyes having different sensitivity to light suggests that one set of eyes could function in daylight, as they do, for a lobster in a tank is immediately aware of a hand approaching him. ★ ★

Lobsters certainly shun light, as is evident in lobster tanks where the lobsters will shrink away from light, and huddle together in the darkest corner.

Experiments with lights for lobster lures have met with little success, confirming the belief that lobsters shun even the dimmest light.[6]

Lobster eyes seem to be affected by agitation. One ★ ★ lobster dealer whose statements are dependable has noticed the color of a lobster's eyes during a storm. He keeps his lobsters in crates in the water, and the crates are naturally tossed around in a storm. At such times, the eyes of the lobsters turn so ruby red that they are clearly noticeable.

Taste and smell. Lobsters have no taste or smell organs in the usual meaning of the words, and it seems probable that these two senses are blended together, and stimulated either by touch or by a chemical reaction. The process is not understood with any exactness. Nearly every part of a lobster's body is subject to these stimulations. The stimulation, whether of touch or chemical nature, is conveyed to the lobster's nervous system by tiny hairs which cover most of its body. They are its most important sense organs. Thus it is that although encased in what seems a solid, impenetrable armor, the lobster can receive stimuli and impressions from without as readily as if it possessed a soft and delicate skin. The dense shell of a lobster is in reality a veritable strainer, being perforated by hundreds of thousands of minute passages which lead from the surface to the sensory nerves that lie at the roots of the hairs. On the shorter antennae these hairs are particularly evident, and the mouth parts are more sensitive than the antennae.

The hairs on the feet of lobsters are sensitive and are an aid to the lobster as it explores the bottom for food, whipping the water with its long antennae, and testing all

---

[6] *See* page 83.

objects with them and its feet. Being dim-sighted the lobster must necessarily sense holes or other unfavorable conditions in the bottom with its feet, and the foot movement is probably quite fumbling in its search for something solid to bear its weight.[7]

The lobster's hairs are tremendously responsive to even very dilute evidences of food, and a lobster will react vigorously to the trail left in the water by a finger which has been in contact with meat.

Even more remarkable is a lobster's reaction to fish ★★ oil spilled on the surface of a shallow ocean pool. There its response can be seen. The lobster will move until it is beneath this oil film and follow it even though the oil is only on the surface and several feet above it.

Hearing. A lobster has no organ comparable to an ear, and probably does not have a sense of hearing. It does sense noise, not as sound but rather as vibrations. Lobstermen in Cohasset agree that they cannot catch lobsters following the explosions of Fourth of July fireworks on nearby Nantasket Beach. Enormous lobsters were caught in New York waters until Revolutionary days. In *Letters From America 1792*, it says, "Since the incessant cannonading lobsters have entirely forsaken the coast; not one having been taken or seen since the commencement of hostilities."

Touch. Touch is the most primitive sense of animals, and in a lobster it is present in the hairs, which also act as taste and smell organs. The antennae are particularly rich in these hairs to record whatever they touch.

Balance. It is commonly observed that while living fish swim with their bodies erect and poised, a dead one floats on its side. The upright position is maintained in life by compensating movements which are automatically called into play by special sensory bodies called static organs. This is true of lobsters, as of all animals which carry themselves

---

[7] *See* page 46.

upright in opposition to gravity. In a lobster, these organs are pockets lined with sensitive hairs, many of which have little weights in the form of tiny sand grains glued to their tips. The grains swing about with the least movement of the body and telegraph their position to the nervous system.

It is possible that the large antennae contribute to ★★ the sense of balance. If both large antennae are cut off and a lobster is balanced vertically on its head in a tank, it will hold this position for several hours.

Molting

The molting of a lobster is a most interesting procedure. The shed shell is often found, and the act itself has sometimes been observed.

A lobster molts because its meat has grown but its inelastic shell has not. A freshly molted lobster will be an inch or more longer than its cast shell.

Molting begins the second day after hatching and continues through the life of the lobster, or at least as long as it is growing. The first three molts are passed in from twelve to fifteen days. In mature lobsters, the male sheds once a year, unless it is very old and slow-growing. A lobster weighing ten pounds will shed perhaps every three or four years. The female usually molts once in two years if she is fertile, otherwise the same as a male. From first to last, the shell is cast in one piece with only a split down the back. In healthy young animals, molting lasts but a few minutes, but the process is striking and at all times it is critical and sometimes fatal.

Certain changes occur in the body of a lobster in preparation for the molt. Among these changes is the absorption into the body of the lobster of much of the lime in its shell along a narrow line in the solid part extending from its beak to the after end. The shell becomes brittle along this line in preparation to splitting open. A most important change is in the flesh of the lobster, which becomes stringy and watery and unpalatable. The large claws shrink, due to the fluid in the claws being withdrawn into other parts of the body, leaving the claws virtually free from blood. Without this withdrawal and consequent shrinkage, it would be impossible for the claw to be withdrawn without rupture. The layer of skin which is to form the new shell begins to take on its distinctive character before the old one is cast, but does not harden to any extent.

As molting approaches, the lobster becomes markedly uneasy; the shell feels hollow, and the color of the joints changes to deep red tints, clearly telling the experienced lobsterman that the molt is imminent. This recognition is important, as no customer wants to receive a rubbery, soft lobster which may molt in transit (and very likely die).

F. H. Herrick states, in *The Natural History of the American Lobster:*

> When the lobster is approaching the critical point of shedding, the back shell gapes away a quarter of an inch or more from the tail. Through the wide chink thus formed, the flesh can be seen glistening, giving it a decided pinkish tinge.
>
> The lobster lies on its side and bends its body in the shape of the letter V. Presently the old cuticle holding the two halves together begins to stretch, and slow but sure pressure finally bursts the skin, revealing the brilliant colors of the new shell.
>
> When this stage has been reached, the lobster becomes quiet for a few seconds and then resumes its task with renewed vigor. The doubled-up fore part of the body, with each effort of the animal, is more and more withdrawn from the old shell.
>
> The solid part of its shell is unbroken, yet the two halves of the shell bend as upon a hinge along a line (from the beak to its after end) where the lime of the shell has been absorbed. No part of the covering of the large claws or of any of the legs has been split or cracked.

The solid part of the shell usually splits open as straight and clean as though it had been cut with a knife.

Fig. 1. The empty, moulted shell

> The muscular masses of the powerful claws are drawn through the small openings at the base of the claw as a wire is pulled through the holes of a draw plate. What this implies can be best appreciated when it is realized that the cross section of the biggest part of the big claw is more than four times greater than at its narrowest point.
>
> The newly molted lobster has a very sleek and fresh appearance and its colors were never brighter or more attractive. Try to take it up in the hand, after some time has elapsed, and it feels as limp as wet paper, and rubbery. Every part of the old shell down to microscopic hair has been reproduced in the new one, but the new shell is so soft that it can be cut with a fingernail. The large claws are considerably distorted, as well as some other parts, being compressed and drawn out to an unnatural length.[8]

In this condition, the newly molted lobster is lean and miserable. It is helpless to protect itself, and is eagerly attacked by cod and by hard-shelled lobsters. It is very likely to be injured and will die if handled at all at this time.

It is interesting that the flesh of soft-shelled lobsters is considered unpalatable, while the edible crab is most delectable just after shedding, i.e., the soft-shelled crab.

Figure I shows a photograph of the cast-off shell of a lobster. It is complete in all details, even the globular surface of the eyeballs; only the split down the shell tells that it has been shed.

The female lobster often has empty egg cases clinging to her abdomen after they have hatched. Molting is the only way she can get rid of these encumbrances.

Breeding Habits

Sex differences. The differences between a male and a female lobster are difficult to see in lobsters viewed from

---

[8] Francis H. Herrick, "The Natural History of the American Lobster," Bulletin of the Bureau of Fisheries, Document 747 (July 13, 1911).

above. It is only when the lobsters are turned on their backs that their differences become evident.

In the male lobster the two swimmerets nearest the carapace (the solid shell) are hard, sharp and bony, whereas in the female the same swimmerets are soft and feathery. The difference is clearly noticeable either by sight or feeling. When the female is impregnated by the male, his semen is deposited in a pocket in the underside of his mate's body. This receptacle appears as a shield wedged between the bases of the third pair of walking legs. Its function is to hold the sperm until the eggs leave the body and are ready for fertilization.

Mating. The female is always impregnated by the male while she is soft shelled, and often within a few hours after molting. When the female is ready to accept her mate it is believed she searches him out. Anderton in *The Lobster* describes the process:

> Two hours after molting, she was seen roaming round the pond and frequently approaching the various shelters, returning regularly and fearlessly to a shelter containing a large male. On approaching the entrance to this shelter the large claws were extended in a direct line with the body and the antennae were thrust within the shelter. After a few moments the beak of the male appeared, the female meanwhile rapidly whipping her antennae across the now projecting beak of the male, which in turn showed increasing signs of excitement, his antennae being whipped very rapidly over the female in the same manner. After an interval of perhaps a minute the male gradually withdrew from his shelter, the female at the same time turning over on her back to receive him. The sexual act took place at once, occupying only a few seconds, the male retiring at once to its own shelter and the female into another. The following day both were observed to be living in one shelter, and they continued to do so, on and off, for several weeks.

The living together does not usually continue except in captivity.

The male at mating is almost always hard shelled. The sperm has great vitality and endures for months, and possibly years. Female lobsters of all sizes from 8 inches upward have been found with hard shell, and even with newly laid eggs, with their receptacles full of sperm.

The sperm remains in the female's body for at least nine months, alive and vigorous until such time as she spawns. To lay her eggs, the female turns on her back and flexes her abdomen into a pocket. The eggs then flow from her genital openings at the bases of the second pair of walking legs in a steady stream into the pocket, passing over the sperm receptacle on the way. At this time the sperm cells leave the receptacle and fertilize the eggs. In this transfer the eggs are attached to the mother's swimmerets by a natural adhesive, to remain throughout the period of incubation.

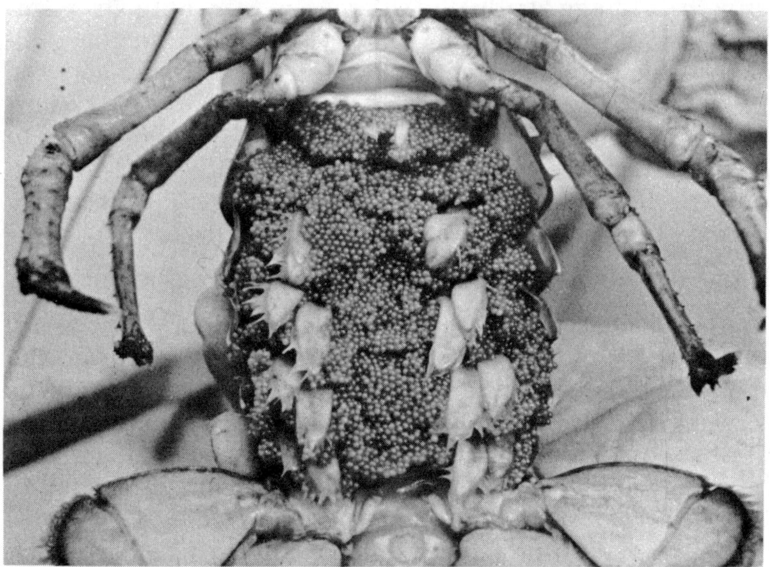

Fig. 2. "Berried" or "seed" lobster

For ten to eleven months the female, now called a "berried lobster"—see Figure 2—constantly guards her eggs against marauding fish and steadily moves her swimmerets to aerate and clean the eggs.

A lobster lays from 3,000 eggs (for a 7-inch female) to 75,000 (for an 18-inch female). Ten thousand eggs is about average for 10-inch lobsters (1¾ pounds). The eggs resemble caviar and are about 1/16″ diameter. Their color, when freshly laid, is a dark green. As they grow old they become lighter in color. This is most noticeable toward the close of the period of development, when the phrase "old" or "light" egg lobster is commonly used by fishermen to distinguish them from the "black" egg lobsters, which have more recently spawned.

The stored yolk of the egg supplies the materials for growth; the egg gradually enlarges in size until its membrane bursts, hatching the young lobster. The mother's instinct is mainly directed to protecting her eggs, and the young disperse as soon as hatched, rising to the surface where they remain into their fourth stage. It is interesting to note that surface-swimming young lobsters seem to be attracted often by light, a trait that is not evident after they become bottom-crawling.

Food

A lobster's food consists mainly of fish, alive or dead, shellfish (clams and mussels), other lobsters and even the skeletons of small lobsters. The bones of fish as well as bits of clam shell are swallowed, and are necessary for building a lobster's shell. In soft-shelled lobsters, the stomach may be crammed with fragments of shell whose lime is needed to harden the lobster's new shell.

Lobsters can probably catch fish alive, particularly such fish as flounders and sculpin, which inhabit the bottom. Lobsters will eat any flesh if they are hungry, from sea-gull to raw beef. They will even enter an unbaited trap, but it is not known whether this is from curiosity, or in seeking a darker retreat, or for some tiny hint of a by-gone bait.

In general, lobstermen prefer an oily fish as bait, the choice being between herring, mackerel, or redfish, the remains of filleted redfish being often available. There are some contradictions to the above statement, since sculpin is considered good bait, yet is not particularly oily. Crabs are used when fish bait is not available, but their shells must be crushed so as to spread the taste and odor of their flesh through the water. They are fair bait but by no means first choice.

Herrick says, "Clams are undoubtedly a favored food as evidenced by the holes dug in the bottom by lobsters in a pound, and by the open broken clam shells abounding."

Lobsters are scavengers, meaning that they will clean up food on the ocean floor, and sometimes their food is too ripe for human taste. Anyone who doubts this has only to examine and smell a barrel of salted herring which has been put down during the summer as a reserve for later fishing, when bait is scarce. It is good bait but not as good as fresh herring. Even so-called fresh bait becomes quite ripe during the several days in summer that it takes to use up a barrel. But lobsters will not touch putrid food. Lobstermen agree that fresh bait fishes best, and they would use it wholly if they could get it, but some think there are times when the riper bait is actually better. They know that lobsters are more fastidious than crabs, which will eat anything even if it is rotten.

Lobstermen do not like the stink of rotten fish any more than anyone else. One lobsterman reported that his wife would not let him sleep with her because he still smelled so badly of fish, even after taking a bath. A further objection is that a decayed fish becomes soft so as to be easily washed or torn off the bait hook. Fish heads are a desired bait because they "hang on" and are not readily torn away.

Since oily fish are a preferred bait, it would seem that the fish oil must be the attractant. Experiments with Lob-Lure, an artificial bait, led to the conclusion that the benefit of oil in a fish bait was because the oil waterproofed the fish flesh, causing it to "hang on" and fish longer, rather than because the oil was so attractive.

There is no evidence that shorts prefer a different bait than do larger lobsters. This statement is based on the records of LobLure, which listed the number of each size caught with each bait.

Any bait that is too decayed becomes "sour" and ★ ★ will not fish at all. Similarly, a netted bait bag will become "sour" after several fishings, and must be scrubbed out and sunned. It will not fish even if loaded with fresh bait.

Most lobstermen believe that a storm will affect a a lobster's feeding habits. They note that even during summer lobsters' appetites seem to fail at times, but that after a storm they will again come into pots. It is thought that the agitation of storm waves shakes them out of their lethargy.

Lobsters need a change in diet. When fishing is poor, a change in the kind of bait will often correct the trouble.

A moderate amount of salt in any bait does not affect its attractiveness.

Fish heads are good bait. And most of the blood of a fish is in its head. Is this significant?

Lobsters need lime from which to build their shells. It is reported by Herrick that a newly molted lobster will eat its own cast, or gorge on shell fragments to replenish this lime. Phosphorus exists in large quantities in lobsters. In hot weather, when a dead lobster ceases to be fresh, it exhibits a highly phosphorescent appearance similar to that of a glowworm. It is probably caused by the chemical changes in the lobster flesh and is a slow combustion by oxygen. Goode reports *(Fisheries and Fishing Industries of the United States):* "The presence of phosphorus in a lobster is of great importance to the consumers of these sea luxuries; there is no substance which conveys phosphorus so readily into the human system in an agreeable form, and which the system so readily and quickly assimilates, as the flesh of lobsters."

Enemies

Herrick lists man as the principal enemy of lobsters. He states that codfish come next, and the stomachs of cod are often stuffed with young lobsters. Raccoons can be a nuisance, and pounds near woods, as at Steuben, Maine, are pestered by coons which come down to the shore at low tide to scoop up lobsters. The woods around such pounds are littered with their shells. Poundkeepers keep a rifle handy, and manage to kill a dozen or more coons each year.

Diseases

Red Tail. During the summer of 1946, an unknown disease became epidemic in many lobster storage pounds along the Maine coast and caused a high mortality among lobsters stored there. The Sea and Shore Fisheries and Maine Agricultural Experiment Station joined forces to investigate the disease.[9]

At the beginning of the investigation, it was believed that this disease of lobsters could be recognized by a creamy pink to red coloration of the underside of the abdomen, thus the name "Red Tail." Later, it was discovered that this red coloration could not be relied upon as a symptom, but since the term Red Tail had become so widely known to designate this disease, no attempt was made to change it.

Only a microscopic indication will prove that the disease is present in lobsters. It shows up in the sharp, progressive increase in weak and dead lobsters among those stored in pounds, cars, and tanks, especially after the temperature of the water has reached 45°F. or higher. The disease was found to be non-poisonous to human beings and other warm-blooded creatures, but highly contagious among lobsters.

This study further showed that while the lobster is its natural host, the disease organism can live and multiply outside the lobster tissue in the slime of lobster tanks, cars, crates, bait barrels, and smack wells; it is also found in the mud of tidal pounds and abounds in the sea water of tanks,

[9] *See* John S. Getchell, "A Study of Red Tail," Maine Department of Sea and Shore Fisheries.

cars, and tidal pounds where the infection is known to be present. With the constant discharge of water from infected storage places into open water, the organism has been traced for miles until the dilution by the sea itself makes detection impossible.

From transmission studies, it has been found that healthy lobsters that have devoured infected, weak, or dead lobsters, and even those that did not have access to diseased tissue but lived in the sea water contaminated with the organism, fell victim to the disease.

Since to eliminate the disease is to remove the Red-Tail organism, and since there is no known cure for the disease once the lobster has become infected, the next best procedure is to attempt to remove the breeding places of the organism and to keep healthy lobsters as far as possible from becoming exposed to the disease. To even attempt this, strict sanitation of all lobster storage places must be maintained.[10]

The true host, the lobster, must be present for the disease to last over a period of time. This is shown by the fact that in the absence of lobster tissue and with continuous flushing by fresh sea water, the organism slowly disappears. It is, therefore, most important that dead lobsters and lobster parts be constantly removed from storage places and destroyed. They should never be disposed of where they may cause a contamination of either artificial or natural habitats of lobsters. Weak lobsters should be considered suspect, especially after the water temperature has reached 45°F., and either be isolated and observed in separate tanks or cars, or disposed of.

To insure minimum loss, it is recommended that tidal pounds should not be stocked during warm weather but at a time when the temperature of the water is 45°F. or below. If, however, tidal pounds must be stocked, the general rule applies. Remove as completely as possible every day, and destroy by burning or burying, all dead lobsters and lobster

---

[10] *See* Pounds, page 111.

parts. Never throw this refuse where it may find its way back into the pound. Never throw it into the ocean, for the organism can be brought back into the pound by the tide or can serve to infect lobsters yet uncaught.

When mortality is on the increase, the remaining healthy lobsters should be removed and either stored in fresh, clean cars, well away from the pound and in well circulating water, or disposed of on the market. Once the pound is empty, the gates should be left open so that it can be flushed by the natural rise and fall of the tide. This operation should continue for at least a week before any attempt be made to restock. Storage tanks, cars, crates, and bait barrels can be cleaned and disinfected with a hypochlorite solution. They must then be well flushed, as chlorine is poisonous to lobsters.

Shell disease. Shell disease in lobsters is caused by a bacterium that attacks the horny part of the shell. The disease appears to attack all parts of the exterior shell, but apparently does not attack the antennae, the mouth parts, the eyes, or the thin membrane between the various body segments.[11]

In advanced stages, the disease is easily recognized by the characteristic eroded appearance of the shell. Large areas of the shell of the tail and carapace may be completely eaten away, exposing the soft inner layer (see Figure 3). The outer edges of the injured parts are characteristically white in appearance and it is in this white area that the bacteria are active.

It is probable that in the early stages of the disease the bacteria lodge in the minute pores of the shell. During the incubation period of the disease, an infected lobster cannot be distinguished from a healthy one. The first evidences of infection are tiny, pinpoint damaged spots (lesions). These injuries are especially difficult to recognize on the walking legs, where they frequently first appear.

---

[11] *See* Clyde C. Taylor, "A Study of Lobster Shell Disease with Observations and Recommendations," Maine Department of Sea and Shore Fisheries Bulletin.

Fig. 3. Shell disease
Reproduced from Sea and Shore Fisheries bulletin "A Study of Lobster Shell Disease."

The disease develops rather slowly, at least three months being required for it to reach advanced stages. Observations on lobsters held at the Boothbay Harbor station indicate that the disease is relatively dormant at temperatures below 35°F., but becomes increasingly active as the water temperature approaches and exceeds 40°F.

Observations up to the present indicate that the disease is spread only through physical contact with diseased lobsters, but experiments are now in progress to determine if it may be carried by water. Horn-decomposing bacteria are known to be widely distributed in nature, and it is possible that the disease may be spread through contact with the mud of infected pounds.

It has been shown that lobsters free from previous contact with the disease will develop it when held in tanks with diseased lobsters. In one experiment, 36 per cent of the healthy lobsters put in tanks with diseased lobsters developed visible lesions in forty days. A mortality of 71 per cent has been observed among diseased lobsters held in tanks for a period of eighty-eight days.

The bacteria in shell disease attack only the external parts of the lobster and exhaust their food supply before ever reaching edible flesh. Although lobsters in the advanced stages of the disease are very unsightly, it has never been reported that the presence of the disease in a shipment impairs the value or marketability of the lobsters.

In order to prevent the spread of shell disease to native lobsters, dealers who handle imported lobsters must be very careful to avoid dumping dead lobsters or parts of dead lobsters from an infected lot into the ocean where native lobsters can come in contact with them. Since it is customary to dispose of dead lobsters by dumping them in the sea, great care must be taken to see that every person handling an infected lot is clearly instructed.

The recommended means of disposing of lobsters with shell disease is to burn them. This is readily accomplished if a coal fire is available. When burning is impractical, boiling for thirty minutes and dumping on a garbage dump is a safe procedure. In one instance, an abandoned, water-filled quarry has proved an effective and inexpensive means of disposal.

We have no record of shell disease developing in a pound containing only Maine lobsters. In every reported case, the disease has been associated with the presence of imported lobsters. This fact is of great significance since it indicates there is no continuity of infection in a pound. The absence of continuity of infection may be interpreted to mean that contamination in the pound disappears during the spring and summer months when the pound is empty and that the disease organism requires a living host.

Although shell disease has been known in Canadian waters since 1936 and in Maine pounds since 1942, there is no evidence that the disease is present in Maine waters except for a few diseased specimens widely scattered both in space and time. It appears probable that the disease is not water-borne. The presence of the disease in adjacent Canadian waters and its apparent absence in Maine waters is a surprising fact, however, and we would be most unwise to conclude that the disease is unlikely to break out in our native stocks. We must consider ourselves fortunate up to the present time and exercise every known precaution to prevent its introduction.

Plug rot. This is a decay and blackening of the claw meat adjacent to the plug. It may proceed so that the shell is decayed away for an area as large as a quarter, exposing a marble-sized section of black, dead meat.

This infection is rare and appears in lobsters which have been held some time.

Plug rot must be blamed on the plug. It is not evident why it appears so infrequently, or what there may be in the way the plug is inserted to make the infection so virulent.

The Sea and Shore Fisheries report that plug rot occurs equally with either wood or plastic plugs, but is most noticeable with the hand-whittled Canadian plugs. These often have a curved shape so that their points fetch up against the inside of the claw shell, and can possibly chafe and irritate.

Gas disease. Gas disease is covered in detail in a paper "The Gas Disease in Lobsters," by Donald M. Harriman, of Sea and Shore Fisheries, who writes:

"Gas disease is caused by super-saturation of air in water. This in turn results in super-saturation of dissolved nitrogen, which is injurious to lobsters." It occurs when a water pump is working against high pressure and there is an air leak on the vacuum side of the pump, usually through the packing. Thus air as well as the water is sucked into the pump.

Gas disease, when acute, will kill lobsters in a matter of hours; when it is not acute, in from two days to two weeks.

Gill disease. The gills of lobsters are sometimes infected with parasites (primarily a British disease). This organism can be seen, when the gill cover is removed, as pinkish, egglike protrusions, up to 1/5″ long, from the gill filaments to which the organism is firmly attached. When present in small numbers, the parasite has no noticeable effect on the lobster, but may, in the case of heavy infestation (several hundred on each side), weaken the lobster. As the organism remains attached to the gills throughout its adult life, and the eggs which are produced cannot, so far as is known, lead to a direct reinfection of lobsters, the parasite cannot be regarded as a potential source of an epidemic amongst stored lobsters.

Bowel movement. The dung of a lobster will kill ★★ other lobsters. That is one reason why lobsters are commonly kept in a tank before shipping out. Thus the bowels can be emptied, and there will be little dung to sift down in a shipping barrel to kill the lobsters in the lower layers.

Sea Fleas

Sea fleas are very much of a nuisance to lobstermen. They can completely eat the bait in a pot in an hour. They are particularly active and numerous during one month in the fall.

LobLure tried to eliminate fleas by lining their cylindrical wire bait container with a fine plastic screening. This would effectively keep out mature fleas, but the tiny young ones could squeeze in, gorge themselves on bait and be so swollen they could not get out. Frequently, a heaping tablespoon of such fleas would be found inside, and no bait.

The refuse (heads, guts, and skin) of smoked ★★ herring is commonly believed to be repellent to fleas. It has the pleasant odor of smoked herring, keeps indefinitely, and is cheap. It can be obtained in Eastport. One elderly lobsterman used it alone as a bait, and claimed it fished as well as brim. He first cooked it up with water and used it in a bait bag. Actual tests showed it to be an inferior bait. It is not known if lobstermen ever mix smoked herring scrap with their regular bait in order to repel sea fleas. It might be helpful.

Measuring a Lobster

In all New England States today a lobster is measured by a metal gauge which hooks into the eye-socket at one end, and over the edge of the carapace (the solid part of his shell) at the other end (see Figure 4).

In Maine and in Massachusetts the legal length for a lobster is 3 3/16 inches.

Maine has also an oversize limit: a lobster which is over 5 inches may not be taken. The idea behind this oversize limit is the belief that the larger lobster will produce more eggs, and thus aid in conservation. This idea is hotly refuted by some lobstermen who claim that the intermediate size lobsters are the greatest breeders due to their greater virility, and they point to many examples in animal life where younger ones are more sexually active. Maine is the only state with this oversize limit.

Mr. Robert L. Dow, Research Director of Sea and Shore Fisheries, points out that it is not true with marine forms

Fig. 4. Measuring a lobster

that more progeny means more adults. " The maximum size limit in Maine was established because the larger sizes would not sell well in the live lobster market, and it was a convincing but spurious argument to offer ' conservation ' as justification for legally excluding these less salable sizes from the catch. This limitation is anti-conservation in that these protected animals [those in excess of 5″ carapace] are not efficient in their use of food which we assume to be of limited capacity, but they are also cannibalistic, and occupy space which might be better used by smaller, more efficient lobsters."

II

Means of Catching

Early practices. The primitive method of catching lobsters was by means of a hooked staff resembling a shepherd's crook. This was thrust into the lobster's hiding place exposed at low tide, and the lobster withdrawn by the hook. For many years on the coast of Norway, lobsters were taken with wooden tongs about twelve feet long and adapted for use in shallow water. All the catch taken by such means were more or less severely injured in the taking, and were unfit for transportation.

The gaffing of lobsters from small boats was a common practice in the early history of the American fishery, and in the period of plenty from 1850 to 1860, a fisherman could take 150 lobsters in a single morning. These devices were followed by the hoop net which consisted of a circular iron ring four feet in diameter, across which netting was loosely stretched to form a bag net (*see Figure* 5). Bait was secured at the center of the net and four ropes secured around the circumference leading into a single rope for hauling the trap. These nets were hauled every fifteen minutes, so apparently the lobsterman had only a few of them, and rowed around tending each frequently. It is an interesting commentary on the plentifulness of lobsters that hoop nets could be effective. The majority of lobsters attracted to the bait would remain on the net during the short periods between haulings. Hoop nets were the common trap up to the time of the

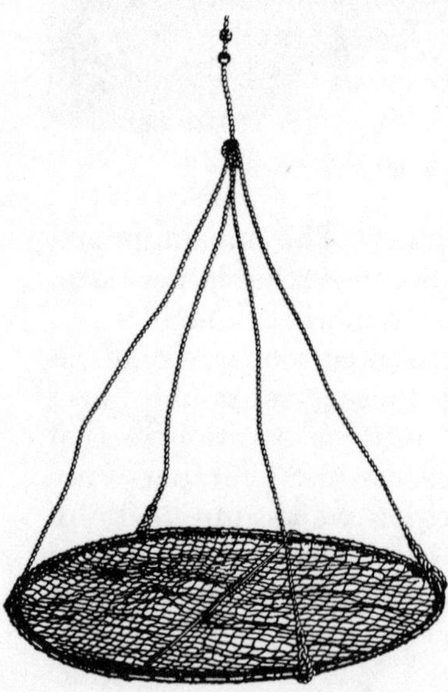

Fig. 5. Hoop net

development of the lobster pot. They are still used in British lobster pounds to fish out the impounded lobsters.

In dense lobster population the hoop net is said to be more efficient than the pot.

The American pot. Although all American pots function the same way, yet it is another piece of lobstermen's gear about which many disagree. Some of the variations in design are:

1. The half-round pot, the earliest style, using black alder bent bows. Modern pots of this style use steam-bent oak bows. It withstands rough handling better than the square pot.
2. The square pot, which is easier to make, and stacks better in the cockpit of a boat.
3. Parlor pots, which doubly trap a lobster. One less knitted head is necessary in non-parlor pots. Most American pots today are parlor ones.
4. Two side entrance openings versus one opening. Here again is a saving of one knitted head. The one-opening pot would seem to be less efficient, for the single opening can be blocked by kelp. Yet some able lobstermen claim they catch just as many lobsters with a single entrance pot.
5. In a few harbors, pots can be found which have two entrances at either end rather than the sides. They do not have parlors. Such pots have to be unusually long. Otherwise, a lobster can reach through the head ring (without actually passing through it) and get at the bait.

Parlor Pots are undoubtedly the most effective type. They do retain more of the trapped lobsters, but they by no means hold 100 per cent of the lobsters caught. To prove this, any lobsterman can put five lobsters in the parlor, leave the pot down overnight, with no bait, and there will be less than five lobsters in the pot the following morning. Some of them will have escaped.

Lobsters seem to be repelled by the acid in new ★★ oak pots. Freshly made pots do not fish well the first

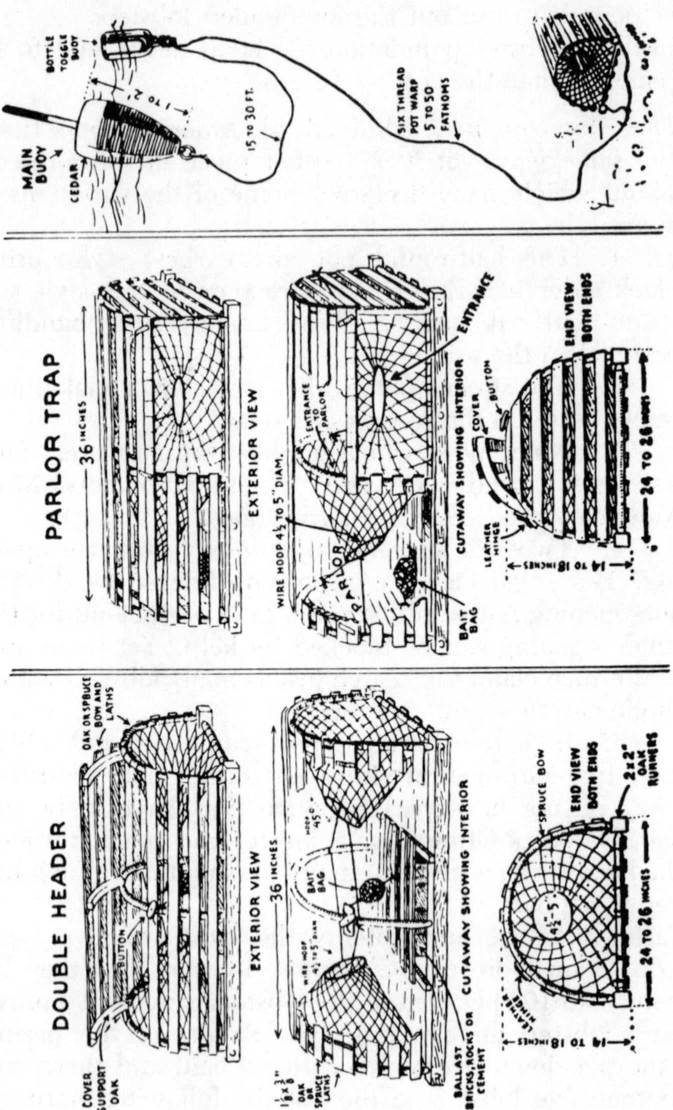

Fig. 6. Traps and buoys

few days, and all new oak pots are soaked underwater ★ ★ for several days. This undoubtedly waterlogs the pots and makes them heavier, but it is probable that much of the acid in the oak is thus leached out.

Heads. One of the few pieces of trapping gear that lobstermen universally agree upon is the use of nylon for the netting of the heads. Only a few years ago, heads were made of marline or other tarred twine. But after World War II, there were quantities of surplus nylon parachute cord which sold at a fraction of their cost. Someone tried nylon out as a header twine, and its strength and durability brought it into general acceptance. There can be quite a difference in nylon cord; some can be bothersome by kinking, and all of it should have the cut ends sealed off with heat, since nylon unlays readily, and does not hold a knot. The braided nylon is used mostly for bait bags. Nylon has been braided over string, plastic filaments, and glass cord in an effort to reduce the cost of the twine. None of the experiments was successful, either because its life was too short or the twine was stiffened so as to make knitting more difficult.

Nylon header twine is made in two weights, and two colors, white or green, and it is amusing to hear how emphatically each lobsterman will defend the greater efficiency of the color he prefers.

In some parts, such as at Martha's Vineyard, the funnels for the heads are made of wood laths. They afford better footing for a lobster than nylon netting, and also can more easily be fitted with a non-escape device, such as a hinged wire across the opening of the parlor head.[1]

Netted heads must be mounted taut or the pot will not fish. This is probably because a taut head furnishes a more rigid footing for the lobster. (An acrobat who is a slack-rope walker has to be more skillful than a tight-rope walker.)

A lobster pot is an excellent example of Yankee inge-

---

[1] *See* page 47.

nuity. It is a simple, practical machine which works; and it uses materials available in out-of-the-way sections of the country. However, except for the development of the parlor pot and the use of nylon header twine, there has been no big improvement in lobster pots for over one hundred years. Where a mechanism has been so long without any great improvements, it seems highly probable that it is open to redesign.

In the old days, lobstermen had to use the materials right at hand, but today with so many new materials available, and with modern transportation permitting these materials to reach the farthest corners, it is time to reconsider lobster pot design.

Criticism of design. There are several objections to the modern lobster pot.

First, it is too heavy for easy handling when out of water, yet not heavy enough to anchor it securely to the ocean floor when submerged. Because the pot is 99 per cent wood, it is buoyant, and most of the ballast in a pot functions to overcome this buoyancy rather than to hold the pot down on the ocean floor. A pot which weighs 44 pounds out of water weighs only 8 pounds submerged. Yet it is a 44-pound lift when the pot is finally hauled out of the water and into the boat. In other words, 36 pounds of the weight of a pot is lost as far as acting as an anchor.

Any redesign of a pot which would eliminate this useless buoyancy would make the job of lobstering much easier. The obvious correction of this fault is to reduce the wood used in a pot. Note the British pot described below.[2] Instead of wood slats, the frame is covered with nylon netting. This, of course, reduces its buoyancy. A pot constructed of metal would also solve this problem, but many lobstermen believe that a metal pot will not catch lobsters. Experiments with metal pots have been made by using galvanized chicken wire in place of slats. Such pots will catch crabs, but seem to repel lobsters.

---

[2] *See* page 45.

This might be because of chemical action of sea ★ ★ water on the zinc used in galvanizing, producing an offensive chemical. Or it might be that ocean currents can vibrate the wire in such a way as to scare the lobsters. The experimental traps described on page 44 have *stiff* metal screening, and they are reported to fish well. However, stainless steel would seem to overcome this objection, and even with galvanized metals the surface can be coated with a plastic skin, which would eliminate the action of sea water on zinc.[3]

The minute a practical pot made of metal is designed, most of the lost weight from the buoyancy of wood will be eliminated, and the weight of the metal in the pot will take the place of much of the present ballast.

Remember that it is the weight per square foot of a pot *underwater* which determines how well it hugs the ocean floor. Thus, if the base of the present pot had half of its area, the pressure per square foot on the ocean floor would be doubled.

A second criticism of lobster pots in use is that the loss of pots each year is amazing and averages close to 33 per cent. This is much too high a loss, and any design which would cut this percentage would not only make lobstering more profitable, but would permit a lobsterman to fish longer at each end of the season, when the heavy storms and loss of pots now make lobstering unprofitable.

To understand why pots are lost, it is necessary to conjecture what happens during a storm. In the first place, it will be recalled by any student of high school physics that the action of waves in a bad storm is a circular action reaching to 60 feet in depth. Since this is a common depth for lobster fishing in summer months, most pots are affected by storms.

During a storm, it is probable that kelp is pressed ★ ★ against the side of a pot, closing the openings between the slats and affording a considerable resistance to the

[3] *See* page 102.

waves. On top of this, the light weight of a submerged★ ★ pot (only 8 pounds) does not afford much grip to the ocean floor. It is probable that a pot is rolled over and over, perhaps winding the warp around itself, until the buoy is drawn under, but in any case permitting the pot to be slammed against the ledges and broken. Notice here that the round tops of many pots tend to assist this rolling action rather than to oppose it.

The following changes in the shape of a pot will help to reduce these losses:

a. Any reduction in the height of a pot from the present 18 inches would reduce the leverage tending to overturn a pot.

b. The construction of a pot with inclined sides like a pyramid would change the side pressure of a wave from an overturning effect into a force pressing the pot down on the ocean floor.

This downward pressure exerted on an inclined surface is akin to the side pressure exerted by a wedge. As anyone can recall, the pressure of a wedge in splitting a log is at right angles to the direction in which the wedge is being driven. The flatter the angle of such a pot, the greater it will be forced down against the ocean floor. A 45-degree angle will turn half the side pressure of a wave into a downward force, and an even flatter wedge will turn more of the pressure downward. Such a design would utilize the force of ocean currents to anchor a pot rather than to roll it over.

The steel pot. The steel pot is being fished experimentally off Portland. It is a parlor, two-side-entrance pot whose sides and bottom are covered with expanded steel, rather than wood slats. The sides slant upwards like the roof of a house. Expanded steel is the material commonly used today as the foundation for plastering instead of lathing. It has diamond-shaped openings. The cut edges of the steel are quite sharp on one side but not on the other. It was found that lobsters would not enter the pot if the side of the expanded metal with the sharp edges was placed ★ ★ outside. This illustrates the sensitivity of lobsters' feet since lobsters will commonly crawl over the outside of any pot before entering. Evidently, the sharp edges were repellent. This pot is reported to be as effective as old-style wood pots. Its cost is not known, but its durability must be far greater than those made of wood.

These pots were originally made with metal netting for heads. It is interesting that they would fish well in 15 fathoms or deeper, but not in shallower water. When the heads were replaced by nylon netting, they would fish at all depths. A deduction from this is that wave action made the wire head vibrate at shallow depths, where the wave action is felt, and that such vibration was repellent to lobsters. This conclusion has been given as a reason why chicken-netting pots (instead of slats) do not fish well.

The plastic pot. Plastic pots have been made in Marblehead, but it is probable that their manufacture has been discontinued, since a request to buy one was not answered. The one seen in York was very crude; the components were not made in a die but hand molded. The plastic pot might be very practical on account of its strength, durability, and resistance to teredos but the gamble of the cost of dies to make them would be great. If a manufacturer could only be *sure* his design was right, he might risk the gamble, but he would still have to face the uncertainty of enough lobstermen accepting it. The individual thinking among lobstermen often handicaps the development of new gear for them.

The British or Scotch pot. This pot is quite similar to our two-side-entrance half-round pot, but without an inner bedroom. It differs in that the side slats are replaced by a nylon netting of about the same opening as we use in our heads. This reduces its buoyancy. It lacks the opening between the lower slats to permit small lobsters to escape *(see Figure 7).* Its greatest difference is in the use of a fine mesh netting on the floor of the head as a sort of catwalk. The

Fig. 7. Lobster creel — side view

British have discovered that a lobster will more readily enter a creel (their name for a pot) if his footing is made easier. It sounds reasonable. Anyone who has watched a dog chase a squirrel into a brush pile and climb up the brush pile in pursuit will be struck by the dog's difficulty in finding a footing—the holes between the branches hamper his locating places to plant his feet. How much harder it must be for a lobster with its dim sight to fumble around in the dark searching for a strand of the header to support him. It is a discovery which our lobstermen should investigate.

Dr. H. Thomas of the Scottish Marine Laboratory in his pamphlet, " The Efficiency of Fishing Methods Employed in the Capture of Lobsters," lists the comparative catches of their standard pot as compared with the same pot equipped with a fine meshed catwalk on top of the head. In nineteen test fishings, the standard pot caught an average of 2.7 lobsters, while the catwalk pot caught an average of 3.9 lobsters. *This is a 44 per cent greater catch*, and the average size of the lobsters in the latter type pot was slightly greater. The actual figures are shown below.

The catwalk material is cord knitted with openings about 5/16″ square, and is apparently laced down to the header net.

The three types of creels tested are described herewith:

1. The *standard* pot—a half-round pot with heads at either end and no parlor. This is like the one in Figure 7, but without the fine mesh catwalk.

2. The standard pot fitted with a *non-escape* device on each head. The device consists of a hinged, freely movable ∩ shaped, galvanized iron wire which at rest lies across the opening of the head. It offers little resistance to entry of the pot, but prevents escape through the head. Such a one-way-passage trap has been used by some American lobstermen but has not come into general use. Possibly the tapping noise made when the hanging tongue butts against the ring of the header may scare lobsters away.

3. The standard pot fitted with a *fine mesh* catwalk lying on the head, as shown in Figure 7. "Twelve of each of these types were used in each fishing in depths down to 15 fathoms. They were fished in trawls of eight pots, care being taken to drop them at the same depth as nearly as possible. The period of fishing being twenty-four hours. The following table shows the catches of lobsters by the three types of pots in each of nineteen fishing."

Catch of lobsters by creel types per fishing

	1	2	3	4	5	6	7	8	9	10	11	12	13	14	15	16	17	18	19	*Average*
Standard	1	2	0	6	3	2	4	3	0	2	2	4	2	3	5	2	4	4	3	2.7
Fine-mesh catwalk	4	1	1	5	4	7	6	4	2	2	2	3	3	2	10	1	6	7	5	3.9
Non-escape	3	1	4	3	3	2	3	5	1	2	4	2	0	4	4	4	6	3	6	3.2

The average catch per fishing by the pot with the fine-mesh catwalk is well above the others. Over 20 per cent better than the non-escape pot, and nearly 40 per cent better than the Standard pot.

A weighted estimate of the overall average length of lobsters is given in respect of each type of pot. The fine-mesh catwalk pot caught slightly larger lobsters.

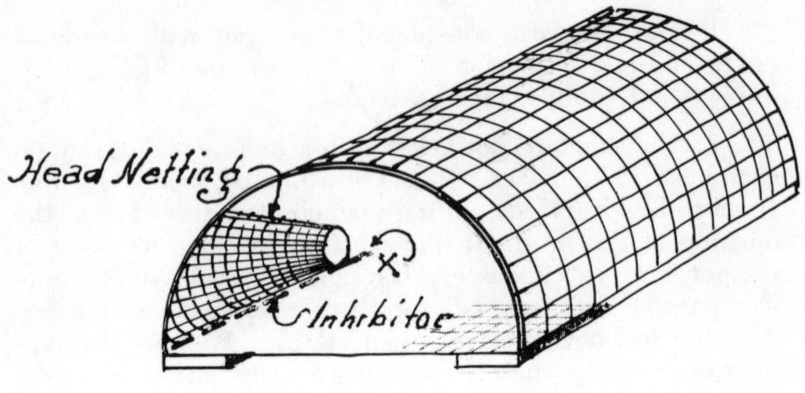

Fig. 8. The Leakey "inhibitor"

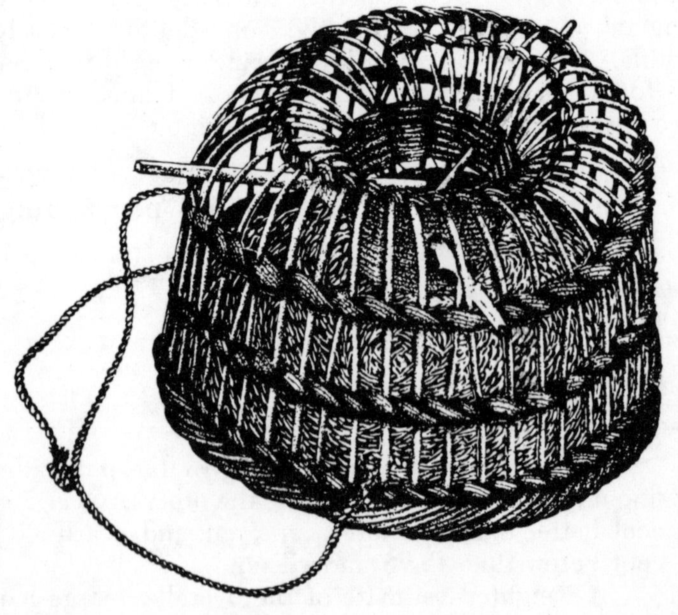

Fig. 9. The Cornish pot

Weighted average lengths in mm. of lobsters caught by creel types

Pot	*Standard*	*Fine-mesh catwalk*	*Non-escape*
Average	276.0	283.2	279.9

Summary. Of the three pot types investigated *those fitted with fine-mesh (5/16") netting onto the lower face of the head inlet caught more lobsters* than did pots not so fitted.[4]

The above tests explain why the sample pot in the bulletin on "Practical Hints for Lobster Fishermen," from the Scottish Home Department shows only a pot equipped with the fine-mesh catwalk as in Figure 7.

The Leakey pot. One of these pots has been imported from England. It is a metal-framed collapsible trap. It is reported that fifteen hundred are in use in Britain. Its bottom and sides are made of nylon netting, and it is held in position of use by a nylon cord which may be readily released or broken by storm damage, allowing the pot to collapse. The hinged door at one end allows the removal of lobsters. It does not have a door in the side to reach the bait hook, and it is not clear how the bait is to be secured. The frame is 3/8" steel rod covered with a protective coating.

The most interesting feature of the Leakey pot is what they call the "escape inhibitor." This is a fine-mesh plastic floor netting such as used on the Scotch pot, but it is stiff and springy, and it extends beyond the opening of the head about 3 inches into the pot, as at X in Figure 8. The inventors state: "The plastic floor extends past the end of the head netting in the form of a row of bristles over which the lobster passes on its way in. If it tries to escape, the bristles not only prod it back but any pressure on them closes the head." It is claimed that Leakey traps can be fished for long periods between hauls without the catch escaping.

[4] H. J. Thomas, "The Efficiency of Fishing Methods Employed in the Capture of Lobsters and Crabs," International Council for the Exploration of the Sea, Charlottenlund, Denmark.

The Leakey pot is reported to be patent pending in the United States.

The Cornish pot. Cornish pots (Figure 9) are similar in shape to the old-fashioned straw beehive. They are built of wicker work, usually from hazel or willow. The flat base is circular of close basket work, of diameter 2′3″. The sides are formed from wands which are brought upwards and then inwards, and finally bound downwards centrally to form an eye at the top of the pot; the height of the pot is 1′8″ and the depth of the eye 7″, its diameter 8″. Wands forming the sides of the pot are at a separation of 1½″ and bound together by a spiral of willow twigs, which generally circle the pot twice in passing from the base to the eye. The eye itself is closely bound by twigs to form a funnel leading into the top of the pot.

Bait is secured in the pot by means of skewers, made of wood and 15″ in length. The bait is fixed to the skewer which is then passed through the mouth of the pot and the point of the skewer is inserted in the close basket work of the funnel, so that the point of the skewer projects downwards and inwards to the centre of the funnel. Generally three such baited skewers are used. The points of the three skewers converge to the centre point of the funnel; sometimes four or even five skewers may be used. Fishermen hold that, providing the closed fist can be thrust into the space between the skewers, ample room is left for the lobster to enter the pot. The skewers not only secure the bait but prevent lobsters escaping from the pot, particularly during hauling.

The following advantages are claimed for the Cornish Pot:

1. They are inexpensive. Hazel or willow wands can usually be collected locally, free.

2. The pots are durable; they withstand sea water and can be walked on when piled in a boat.

The Cornish Pot is used on the English coast from Hampshire around the south and west coasts to Cumberland. They vary considerably from area to area in their dimensions, and in the size of the eye. The dimensions given above refer to the type of pot used in North Cornwall.[5]

The French pot. This is a barrel-shaped pot (Figure 10) constructed of chestnut wood, and is used by many French fishermen, especially for the capture of the spiny lobster. Again, the local abundance and cheapness of the material is the principal deciding factor; also the spiny lobster, like the crab, is held to be very destructive to twine.

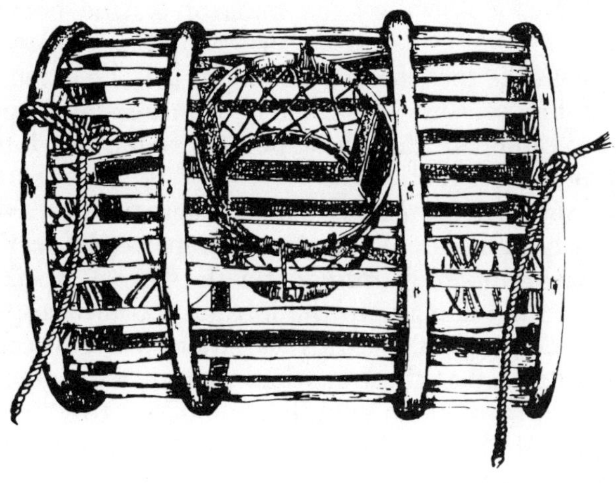

Fig. 10. The French pot

Unlike other traps, the French pot rests on a rounded surface. It is barrel-shaped and weighted to lie on its side. This, it is claimed, lessens the risk of the trap becoming fast between rocks, particularly in areas of ground swell; thus relatively few are lost.

The Dutch pot. It has been stated that lobsters and crabs are repelled by metal. Nevertheless, the Dutch fisher-

[5] H. J. Thomas, *Ibid.*

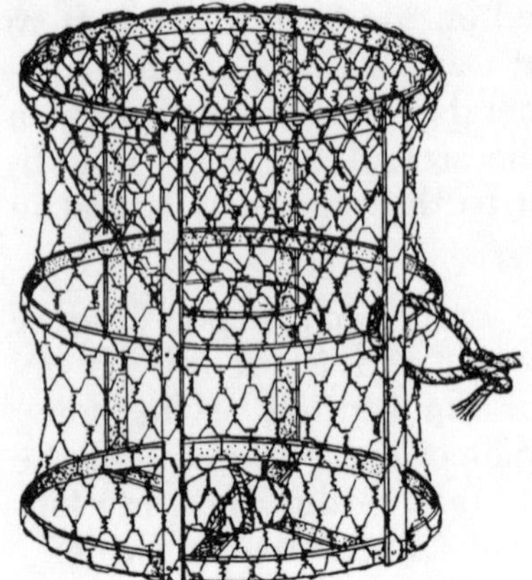

Fig. 11. The Dutch pot

men use a pot (Figure 11) made of galvanized iron wire on a framework of metal, and this seems to fish successfully. The Orkney fishermen do not appear to be at any disadvantage from the use of iron hoops and from the galvanized wire used to form the ring of the eye and eye-shutter.

Care of Pots

Marine borers. The inroads of marine borers are a serious problem to lobstermen, for it is possible that the wood in a pot may be eaten away in less than one season. It is a curse of increasing importance, and would indicate that these borers are moving into northern waters.

A fisherman of Frenchboro (where the ravages were particularly bad) " found that new traps set off in February 1950 were completely riddled by the last of April."

The actual damage to the lobster pot laths appeared to vary. In all probability, this variation was caused by the length of time that the traps had been used. In the tested traps the laths were so completely riddled that only a thin shell of wood fiber held them together. It was impossible to pick up the trap by means of the laths. Squeezing the laths in one's hand produced much the same effect as squeezing a water-soaked sponge.

Although Long Island fishermen were using spruce laths with oak runners, some of them reported that oak did not seem to be any more resistant to the borer than did spruce. It was observed that the oak runners were badly riddled, although perhaps due to their greater volume, they were still in more serviceable condition than were the spruce laths. Experimental traps fished in the Stonington area in 1951 confirmed this observation.

In closely related species, it has been shown that no one of the following: water, temperature, salinity, hydrogen ion content, dissolved oxygen, pollution, and turbidity, is the determining factor in increasing borer population with its consequent increased timber destruction. It has been suggested that a favorable combination of some or all of these factors is what determines an increase in borer population and activity.

Some information is available now on the borer from investigations made elsewhere as well as observations made by the Department of Sea and Shore Fisheries in Maine. It appears that the borer, at the end of its early swimming stages, attaches itself by means of its threadlike filaments to wood. The spawning activity of these organisms is greatest during cold weather, though spawning seems to be influenced by age, and some young are in the water during all seasons of the year. As the borer's shell forms, it works its way beneath the wood surface, where it establishes its protective burrow. Once the borer has established itself within the burrow, it grows rapidly and enlarges its home by rasping away the wood with the hind end of its shell. It may seem surprising that a mollusk as relatively large as a mature borer could have gained entrance to its burrow through a hole as small as that appearing on the wood surface.

Whether or not the borer gains any nourishment from the wood is not entirely clear. Closely related species some years ago were believed to depend entirely on siphonable water-borne food for their nourishment, but more recent studies indicate the likelihood that a portion of their food is derived from the wood they grind up in establishing and enlarging their burrows.

Preservatives. A survey of the literature concerning prevention of damage to lobster pots by marine borers led to three possible methods of attack; namely, the sheathing of all wood with metal, the use of various paints or preservatives known or felt to be repulsive or poisonous to borers, and finally, the construction of traps with metals or plastics not subject to borer attack. The first of these possible methods was deemed impractical and the third is still in the experimental stage, though with some degree of reasonable results. Therefore, this section deals only with the various wood preservatives readily available or easily compounded.

Experimental fishing with treated traps was first commenced on August 11, 1950, and terminated on September 24, 1951. During the period a total of 6,869 lobsters was caught. Two thousand, nine hundred and fifty-nine, or 43.1 per cent, of these lobsters were caught in the treated traps and 3,910, or 56.9 per cent, in their corresponding untreated controls.

In order that a reliable index of catchability might be maintained during the experiment, a treated trap was paired with an untreated trap, in order to reduce to a minimum the influence that varying fishing conditions might have upon apparent catchability results.

Since many commercial lobster fishermen are of the opinion that the treatment of traps would reduce their catchability, experimental traps were built by the Department of Sea and Shore Fisheries; and arrangements were made for several fishermen to operate them in conjunction with their own untreated traps. In this way, it was hoped that practical information on the preservative qualities of various treatments and the effect of these treatments on the catchability of the traps could be obained.

These results can be used only to compare the catchability of one treatment with the catchability of the corresponding untreated control traps. The results are:

In terms of the period covered and the areas fished, it appears that all treatments reduced the catchability of lobster traps.

Treatment	*Treated Traps: Lobsters Caught*	*Untreated Controls*
Creosote dip	168	
Creosote and pitch	274	
Cuprinol	205	Average
Copper paint	273	
Gymseal	316	
Shellac	284	Catch
Pressure creosote	162	
Chromated Zinc chloride	220	
Aniline dye	281	326
Koppers preservative	296	
Intertox	245	
Tar	309	

If 4.7, the average percentage catch of the controls, is used as the catchability index for untreated traps, the following indicates the comparative catchability for the several treatments and materials used in descending order of catchability:

Untreated traps	4.7
Gymseal	4.6
Tar	4.5
Koppers preservative	4.3
Aniline Dye	4.1
Shellac	4.1
Copper paint	3.9
Creosote and pitch	3.9
Intertox	3.5
Chromated Zinc chloride	3.2
Cuprinol	2.9
Creosote dip	2.4
Pressure impregnated creosote	2.3

Although the results of these tests should not be considered absolute, Messrs. Dow and Baird state, they believe the following conclusions are reasonable:

1. The average cost of treatment is sixty cents. The average time consumed in treatment is thirty-five minutes.

2. Borer damage is at least nine times greater in untreated traps than in those that have been treated.

3. The life of any trap will be greatly increased by treatment to prevent borer damage. However, where high losses of traps from storms and other conditions occur, these causes may outweigh the benefits of treatment.

4. Any treatment used seems effective.

5. Treatments applied by brush should be renewed periodically; probably once a year at least.

6. Creosote base preservatives appear definitely to reduce the catchability of the trap.

7. No treated trap was as fishable as untreated traps. (Any copper compound such as Cuprinol is strongly poisonous to lobsters.)

8. On the basis of these experiments, the best treatments are tar, Koppers preservative, and aniline dye.

9. Borer control can be effected to a considerable extent by rotating untreated traps. If untreated traps are removed from the water for a three-day period each month, any borers therein will be destroyed.[6]

Plugs

Lobster claws in Denmark are fastened by a wire; in Britain they are tied with a string.

In the United States plugging is divided between excellent machine-made wooden plugs (basswood) and plastic plugs. The plastic plug came into acceptance due to the fact that claw blackmeat (caused by all plugs infecting the meat) adheres to a plastic plug during cooking and is removed with the plug. Sea and Shore Fisheries, in a bulletin "Lobster Plugs and Their Effect on the Meat of a Lobster's Claw," by Frederick T. Baird, Jr., states: "Discolored ma-

---

[6] *See* Robert L. Dow and Fred T. Baird, Jr., "Methods to Reduce Borer Damage to Lobster Traps," Maine Department of Sea and Shore Fisheries Bulletin #3, used in preparing this section on care of pots.

terial was found to adhere to a plug made of cellulose acetate so that all, or nearly all, the discolored material was withdrawn from the claw with the plug. No other plug tested possessed this characteristic to any degree. This plug is recommended as a means of diminishing the amount of discolored material in the claw following withdrawal of the plug after cooking."

Black infected claw meat is repulsive in the cooked lobster, and many of the largest buyers recognize that this unappetizing black meat reaching the dining table will have an adverse effect on marketing.

Plugging the claw is not done primarily to protect the housewife. It is done to prevent one lobster from injuring another, even to the extent of completely cutting a lobster in two. A lobster is fighting mad and more than usually pugnacious when he is taken out of the water. Usually only the big, crusher claw is plugged. Figure 12 shows how this plugging is done. It requires a little skill to prevent the un-

Fig. 12. Plugging a lobster

plugged claw from nipping the lobsterman's hand while he is inserting a plug.

Many of the Canadian plugs are hand whittled. Some of them are of a fine shape, others not so good. Whittling is a winter pastime there, or a means of obtaining tobacco money for older men. It is estimated that a whittler can make less than 10 cents per hour.

It is commonly believed that plugs made of cedar ★ ★ will kill a lobster—presumably due to the oil in cedar.

Manufactured wood plugs, each branded with the word " Maine " were tried. They were made in the form of a card, like old-fashioned sulphur matches, one to be broken off from the card at a time. They did not meet with lobstermen's approval, and their labeling of a lobster seemed to be of little appeal (see Figure 21).

Bands

The use of heavy rubber bands to secure a lobster's claw has been tried. Ten years ago, the Maine Development Commission even furnished these bands carrying a plastic rectangle on which was printed " Maine Lobster." They were hard to apply; even though some lobstermen developed a sort of scissors to expand the bands, they were still difficult to slip over the claw of an active, pugnacious lobster (see Figure 18).

Today (1961), rubber bands are again being promoted. They are of particular appeal for use on lobsters that are to be pounded. Whether you, as a lobsterman, like it or not, this method is being accepted.

There are several reasons why.

1. A band does not wound a lobster, and an uninjured claw will not become infected. Black meat caused by the infection of a plug cannot occur.

2. If a plug comes out of a claw, the lobster is likely to bleed to death. There is no damage if a band is lost.

3. A plug jammed into a claw at the wrong angle can cause a lobster to " shake " a claw, particularly in cold weather.

4. An article by D. G. Wilder and D. W. McLeese of the Fisheries Research Board of Canada shows that plugged lobsters are more susceptible to the agent causing blood disease.

The first of these reasons is the most powerful. The promoters of bands have addressed themselves to big city buyers who in turn have specified that their purchases be banded. Recently a seacoast buyer was offered an order by a chain store for 80,000 pounds of lobsters (which he had) but his fishermen were not educated to using bands, and the store wouldn't accept his plugged lobsters.

There are two objections to banding. One is that bands cost much more than plugs; an even more important obstacle is the resistance of lobstermen to any new operation.

Excellent tongs are available but they are expensive, and usually the buyer has to provide them free to his fishermen. If a buyer has from twenty to sixty lobstermen fishing for him, the investment in tongs can be considerable.

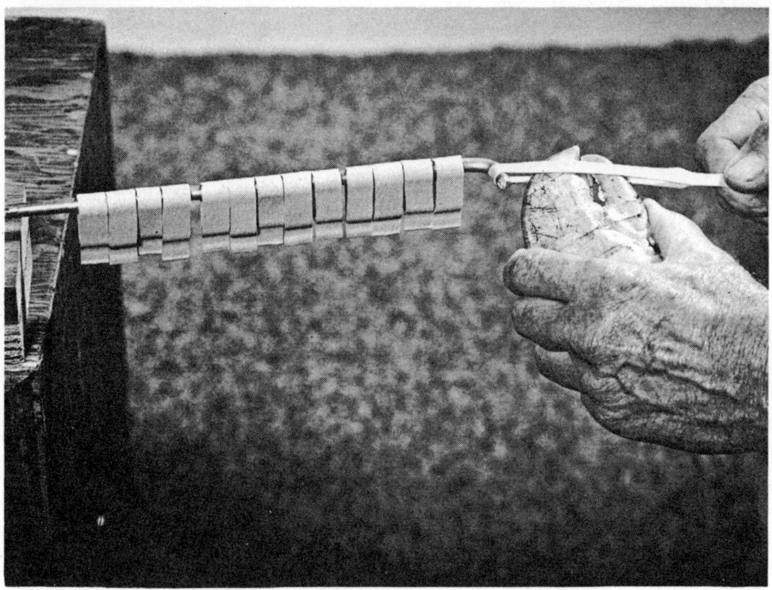

Fig. 13. Banding with tabbed bands

And they do get lost overboard. To meet this problem one lobsterman has worked out a hooked rod as shown in Figure 13. Any fisherman can make one. This device holds about twenty bands strung on it as a magazine. The end band is slid over the hooked end, grasped and pulled outward to receive the lobster claw. This device is a ¼-inch brass rod (which can be bent cold). One end is bent down for 1½ inches to fit into a hole in the cabin top, etc. The other end is bent either upwards or sideways (as it is above) for ⅝-inch. The sideways bending presents the stretched band in a position many lobstermen find most convenient.

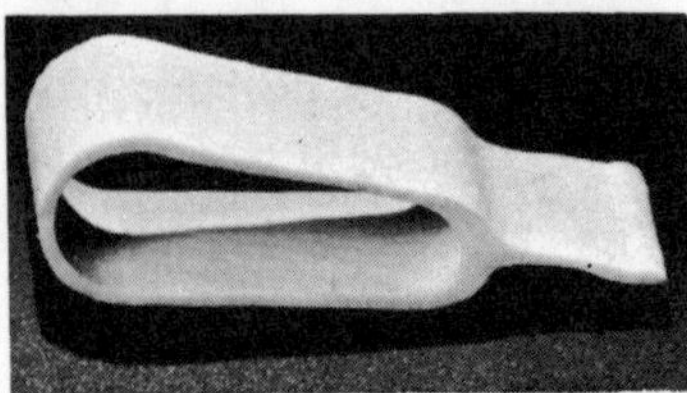

Fig. 14. Tabbed rubber band

Notice that the bands in Figure 13, and the one shown separately in Figure 14, have a tab as part of the band. This tab has proved to be a great aid in using the hooked rod described above. It makes the gripping and stretching of the band much easier. Tabbed bands are the same price per pound as the regular ones. But there are fewer to the pound.

Opinion seems to be equally divided between the lobstermen who claim banding is as quick as plugging, and those who say banding is much slower.

There are two things to look for in buying bands:

1. Don't buy bands made of compounded rubber, even though they are much cheaper. Compounded rubber has been adulterated with cheapening materials. It has neither the stretch nor the life of pure gum rubber. It is easy to test, for compounded rubber will sink if dropped in a glass of fresh water, while pure rubber will float.

2. Don't buy bands less than 7/16″ wide, and ½″ is best. They will stay on better, and be slower to chafe through. The only advantage to a narrower band is that there are more to a pound.

Lobstermen sputter when required to band their catch, and blame the dealer. But there isn't much a dealer can do if his wholesaler demands banded lobsters. In ports where dealers had to have banded lobsters, the fishermen seem to have accepted the change with less opposition than was expected.

The rubber people claim there are approximately 800 regular ½″ bands to one pound.

Buoys

The great majority of buoys are made of white cedar, though white pine ones are occasionally seen. There is need for a better buoy, since even any light wood becomes waterlogged before the season is finished, requiring drying out on the beach. Unfortunately, they do not dry thoroughly, as their paint prohibits exuding all the interior moisture. A glass globe buoy such as is used on nets is a good example. If a glass buoy has a tiny, invisible hole it will leak water inside, yet if hung up indoors, it will retain this water for years.

The war surplus doughnuts of black floatation material made good buoys, but they have all been bought up. Buoyant materials of blown-up plastic are available and good, but they are fragile and expensive.

An ideal buoy

1. has great buoyancy
2. does not become waterlogged
3. is tough
4. cannot be punctured, as by gash from a vessel's propeller
5. takes paint readily

The fluorescent paints, such as Day-glo, could be of benefit to buoys. Buoys painted with Day-glo can be seen much more readily in fog or overcast weather. It is the paint often used on roadside billboards and the tops of fire hydrants. Objections to it are that it is expensive, and it requires a base coat of white paint, then two coats of color and finally a coat of special varnish for protection.

The use of toggles is more common in eastern Maine, where tides run higher than they do to the westward. Toggles are 2-quart glass bottles sealed with a rubber cork (so the water pressure will not push the cork into the bottle) and attached part-way down the warp. They serve to keep the slack of the warp off the bottom at low water. They are a nuisance to handle when the warp runs up over the block in the davit during hauling.

Trawling

Trawling for lobsters commenced about 1955, and was started because of the need of an imaginative dealer who sought for new sources of lobster supply. Lobster buying is highly competitive, and finding a new way to procure lobsters should be profitable.

William Benson of Portland, who was a pioneer in trawling states:

> We use the otter trawl such as is part of a modern dragger, and our nets are employed with exactly the same principles as those of conventional dragging. We have several adaptations which facilitate use of the gear for lobsters especially. For instance, we have to be careful not to crush or damage them. Therefore, we cannot use rollers under any circumstances.
>
> Depths run from forty-three to two hundred and twenty-five fathoms in our experience. Lobsters are most commonly found on the edge of the Continental Shelf in a general area reaching from George's Bank to the Virginia Capes. We fish where experience shows lobsters to have been according to our records. Seasonal movements in locality and depth are predictable.
>
> We do not get many salable fish. Fish do not seem to want to hang around places where there are lobsters. As a matter of fact, lobsters must be downright unfriendly because it is very seldom that you catch anything else when there is good lobster fishing.
>
> We have little or no damage from the nets because of the above mentioned adaptations and precautions. Other mortality averages about three per cent.

The obstacles in the taking of lobsters offshore by this method may be summed up in one thought. The trick is to get them home in good condition.

Damage to gear is rather slight under normal circumstances because we work usually on smooth bottom. A boat adequate for the work and fully equipped would cost a minimum of forty thousand dollars. About ten or eleven units start this type of fishing every year and run into difficulties keeping the lobsters to get them ashore. A lobster is a very complex live, perishable commodity and fishermen with no experience in handling them usually have many troubles.

The future of offshore lobster work is potentially large. It goes without saying that the United States has to expand its fishery in every possible direction to meet competition. It is my opinion that the lobster industry and its methods of production up to this point is the most retarded segment of our coastal industries. The lobster trap we are using today was designed in about 1670. I simply felt there was no sense in waiting another two hundred and ninety years and besides I didn't have the time.

Trawling is not wholly seasonal, and lobsters can be taken in winter. Remember that in a dragging operation we catch what is in the path of the drag, and in trap fishing the lobster has the power of selection as to whether or not he will enter the trap. Lobsters stay in greater depths in winter, and they tend to drop off the Continental Shelf into depths not convenient even for a trawl.

The weight per lobster is much greater than in pot fishing and there are not many shorts. However, one must take into consideration that lobsters travel by sizes. In other words, large lobsters seem to stay by themselves and so do the small ones.

The troubles of learning were many. Keeping the lobsters after we caught them was the biggest hurdle.

We were forced to work in tributaries of the Gulf Stream where water temperatures at the surface were as great as eighty-three degrees. It took a year to devise mechanical means of sustaining the lobsters aboard a boat. Now we can keep them indefinitely. We make trips varying in length five to eleven days.

Because trawling catches many lobsters oversize and illegal for Maine, there is a problem in handling them. It is not necessary for the trawler to go to a port in some other state to unload the bigger lobsters: They can be landed in Maine under bond so long as they are immediately transported out of the state.

There is a feeling among some dealers that really large lobsters are difficult to sell. They contain so much meat that few customers can use them, and often the dealer has to cook them and cut them up to get his money back. Some customers have a belief that the meat of extra large lobsters is tough. This is probably an error, and in any event many epicures feel that such meat has more flavor.

Very large lobsters are a good advertising exhibit when shown alive in a tank.

William C. Schroeder of the Woods Hole Oceanographic Institution has published a pamphlet on trawling that adds much information. The following information is drawn from it:

To the west and south of New England, the landings of lobsters taken offshore with otter trawls have shown a steady increase in the New York-New Jersey region during the past few years. These catches, compared with those taken inshore with pots, show almost two to three times as many lobsters taken by trawl than with pots (1954-1956).

The tagging of lobsters from offshore depths, and their recapture, indicates that these deep-water lobsters do not wander far from their home. This implies that the offshore lobsters live apart from the inshore ones, and furnish a new lobster fishery which as yet has scarcely been touched.

Experiences of fishermen trawling offshore have

shown that an area yielding a good catch one week may be sparsely populated the next, but soon thereafter may again be productive. In such a case, the poor fishing might be due to the large catches of the previous trip, but if so, certain areas, at least, soon become repopulated by lobsters which shift ground, presumably from close by. [This is contrary to records of pot fishing in shallower waters.]

While the offshore population comprises lobsters of all sizes, individuals of two pounds or more make up a much larger percentage of the population than in inshore waters where the fishery has been intensive for many years. . . . Individuals of fifteen to twenty-five pounds are not rare in offshore waters. . . . [7]

The preserving of the catch on the 60-foot dragger *Sonia* was accomplished by "the use of three storage containers on deck (two of them 3 feet wide, 2½ feet deep, 12 feet long, each holding 1600 pounds of lobsters, and one 3 feet by 2 feet by 7 feet, holding 800 pounds) supplied with running water from two pumps. When these were filled, lobsters were packed in the hold on burlap and ice."[8]

Lobstermen are often at war with trawlers, particularly with such trawlers as plow through an area marked by lobster buoys and dredge up the pots and even scrape off the bottom feed. It is probable, however, that trawling as described by Benson, in water too deep for pot fishing, does not hamper the lobsterman.

British Practices

Everyone can learn something from how the other fellow practices his trade. The Scottish Marine Laboratory has researched and reported on customs in the British lobster industry in a detail that we have not reached in this country:

---

[7] William C. Schroeder, "The Lobster, *Homarus americanus,* and the red crab, *Geryon quinquedens,* in the offshore waters of the western North Atlantic."

[8] Ibid. Appendix.

Modern traps consist of some sort of cage with an access via one or more "eyes" [or heads]. They fall into two broad classes; those with an eye at the top which, for convenience, are being referred to as "pots" (examples being the Cornish, French and Dutch pots), and those with a single eye or two eyes situated at the sides, referred to as "creels" and commonly employed around Scotland and Canada, as well as elsewhere.

A test was carried out in Orkney waters on the relative efficiency of the Scottish creel [as in Figure 7], and the Cornish pot [Figure 9]. The two traps were found to be roughly equally effective as judged by the number of lobsters and crabs caught. The creel took 66 lobsters and 91 marketable sized crabs compared with 48 lobsters and 86 crabs in the pot. The Cornish pot, however, took a slightly larger average size of crab than the Scottish creel. The average widths were 5.5″ and 5.2″ respectively.

A proportion of lobsters and crabs which have entered a trap, escape again through the eye(s). It is reasonable to suppose that escape is harder from a pot than from a creel. This however, is offset by the fact that, in practice, the eye of the pot is larger and it is probably for this reason that in the experiments referred to above, the pot retained larger crabs than the creel. It has been suggested that a pot has an advantage over a creel on fishing grounds which have thick growth of long tangle, it being assumed that in these circumstances the low-lying eyes of the creels will become blocked. Against this, however, must be placed the fact that under most conditions the creel eyes are probably more readily reached.

Pots are constructed with a single entrance. Creels, on the other hand, may be single or double entrance. Experiments have shown that the double-entrance creel fishes better than the single entrance. In the test the double-entrance creel caught 62 lobsters and 356 marketable crabs, as compared with 56 lobsters and 280 crabs for the single-entrance creels. This result, however, may not apply in all circumstances. Direct observations have shown that access to a creel offers some difficulty. Lobsters have been seen to hunt around and over the creel, in trying to reach the bait, and often only after some time is access found via the head. In a proportion of cases, access was not obtained. In these circumstances two entrances would seem to increase the opportunity for lobsters and crabs to enter the creel. Furthermore, where a single-entrance creel falls on an uneven bottom, there will be times when the entrance is blocked. On the other hand, the entrance also affords a means of escape. If, instead of being hauled daily, creels are left out for several days at a time, as may be necessary on exposed coasts, it could be that the single-entrance variety would not be at the same disadvantage, compared with the double-entrance type and its double chance of escape. Single-entrance creels can also be constructed in a smaller size than double-entrance and where the number of traps which can be worked is restricted by the size of the boat, it may be advantageous, for lobster fishing, to use the maximum number of the smaller single-entrance creels.

The size of entrance varies considerably. As stated above, the pot entrance is, in general, bigger than that of a creel. For instance, the eye [head] of the French pot is about 10″ in diameter while that of the Cornish pot is about 8″. These compare with an average diameter of 5½″ for the Scottish creel. There tends to be, however, a fairly wide variation about these means. Experiments with the Scottish creel have shown that the diameter of the eye imposes an upper limit on the size of lobsters and crabs which can enter. Crabs are less able to maneuver through a small opening than lobsters of comparable weight and therefore a larger eye is generally required for crab as opposed to lobster fishing. This shows up in the results of experiments using a variety of eye diameters. The size of crab caught is related to the diameter of the eye, much more markedly than is the case with lobsters. In the test, the average length of lobster caught by creels of eye diameter 4″ was 10.6″ as compared with 10.8″ for creels of 6″ eye diameter. In the case of crabs the comparable carapace widths were 5.2″ and 5.6″ respectively. The results obtained, however, depend to some extent upon the stock composition of the populations being fished. For instance, on grounds where the lobsters are mainly large, the size restriction of the creel eye would be more apparent than with a well fished stock where few lobsters were over 12″ overall length. The deterrent effect to larger lobsters of a small sized creel eye has been shown in an experiment comparing the catch of a hoop net with that of a Scottish creel, since there is no size restriction with a hoop net. Using a creel with an eye of diameter 4½″ there was a progressive falling off in the efficiency of the creel vis-a-vis the hoop net in respect of lengths of over 10½″, while for lobsters of lengths 12½″ to 14″ the creel proved little better than half as efficient as the hoop net when comparing the number of large lobsters caught by each gear with the catch of 100 lobsters of 10½″ and under.

Very small lobsters can escape from traps between the meshes or laths. Larger sizes may escape through the eye. While a large eye facilitates entry, it also facilitates escape, and the two effects tend to offset each other. Also, smaller lobsters and crabs escape more readily than larger ones. The interplay of these factors has been shown to result in a larger average size of lobsters being landed from single-entrance creels than from creels with two eyes of the same size, when hauled daily. The effect, however, could well vary according to the fishing conditions, for example, the necessity to leave creels out two or more days.

It has been shown that lobsters and crabs enter a creel more readily if the lower half of the eye inlet is lined by fine mesh netting. The rig of the eye has been found to affect the ease of escape and a high rigged eye has been shown to be the more efficient, particularly with smaller lobsters and crabs which find it less easy to escape. This had the result that the average size of lobster and crab landed was less in the case of the high rig than the low rig. However, this was offset by the greater numbers of lobsters and crabs. It is reasonable to assume that the effect would become more marked as the interval between haulings increases.

The necessity for a larger eye for crabs as opposed to lobster fishing has already been mentioned. This applies also to the fishery for spiny lobsters, and accounts for the very much wider eye diameter (about 10″) used in the French pot. These traps are normally hauled every few hours and are less efficient if employed in the manner usually adopted with creels. It is this type of circumstance, dependent upon local custom, which accounts for the disappointing results some fishermen have obtained when using gear with which they are unfamiliar and which may not be suitable to the particular nature of their fishery.

In some areas where large creels are used in the crab fishery the heads are located in each end of the creel as opposed to the normal position in the sides. They are also made short, the argument being that the end heads facilitate entry into the creel. This is satisfactory for crabs although not for lobsters. The latter, being longer, can reach the bait, which is in line with the eye, without fully entering the creel.

Because of the ease with which lobsters and crabs escape through an open eye, fishermen have developed a number of ways of impeding exit. These, however, must also to some extent hinder entry. The balance between these factors is largely determined by other fishing conditions. The eye of the Cornish pot is protected by three, or sometimes two, skewers which are forced through the basket work of the eye so as to project downwards and inwards towards the centre. The skewers also carry the bait. Creel eyes are often made without any firm inner ring or with the inner end attached to a sleeve of rubber cut from an old car inner tube. The flexible inner end is thought to deter escape.

The most common non-escape device associated with creels is a ∩ shaped wire shutter, hinged to the inner end of the eye so as to open inwards. This device was investigated by comparative fishing experiments. In one series of experiments, using creels of intermediate rig with an eye diameter 4½″, those having non-escape (shuttered) eyes caught fewer lobsters and crabs than open-eyed traps. The respective catches were 56 lobsters and 280 marketable crabs compared with 75 lobsters and 374 crabs for the open-eyed creels. In fact, with the eye in the intermediate position, the deterrent to entry more than offset the limitation of escapes. Creels, however, with low-rigged eye inlets fished better having a shuttered eye. In a second series of experiments, using a light-gauge wire for the shutter and with constant attention to ensure free action of the eye, the non-escape shutter proved advantageous on creels of eye diameter 5″ and over, even though high rigged. Again, at 5½″ eye diameter the respective catches were 22 lobsters and 41 crabs with the open eye as compared with 48 lobsters and 54 crabs with the shuttered eye. But, because of the selective effect of creel eye on the escape of lobsters and crabs, a smaller average size is landed from shuttered-eye creels. For all that, the shutters do not wholly prevent escapes through the eye. Where creels are tilted on an uneven bottom, one eye may be effectively open while the other is obstructed. Also, in dropping a creel, a shutter occasionally gets caught up on the braiding of the top of the creel and the eye therefore remains open. The advantage of any such non-escape device is increased where creels are frequently left for long periods between hauling.

The diameter of the eye and the rig of the eye inlet affect the number and size of lobsters and crabs landed as does the fitment of non-escapement devices. Furthermore, these effects differ with stocks of lobsters and crabs of different size composition and vary with changes in fishing conditions. To achieve the best result the creel should be matched to the circumstances in which it is to be used.[9]

The escape inhibitor of the Leakey pot seems to ★★ overcome some of the disadvantages of the wire shutter.[10]

The size of traps used for catching lobsters and crabs varies considerably. The braided creel, in use around Scotland, has a base diameter of roughly 27″ x 18″ and a height of 14″. Generally this is the smallest type, principally because it can conveniently be constructed in a small size. Traps made in wood, for instance, slatted creels (dimensions 36″ x 22″ x 16″) and Cornish (base diameter 27″, height 20″) or French pots (length 28″, diameter 20″), are larger mainly for ease in construction. It is significant that the Dutch pot, which is in metal, is considerably smaller than the basically similar Cornish pot, which is made from willow. There is, in general, a preference for a larger trap where crabs rather than lobsters are an important constituent of the catch. This is mainly because crabs are often caught several per trap (exceptionally as many as 20 have been taken in one creel) and more room must be allowed than in the case of the lobster, which is much less abundant.

Apart from allowing enough room for the catch, there would appear to be material advantage in adopting a small trap. Its size and small weight make it easy

---

[9] Taken from Dr. H. J. Thomas, "A Comparison of Some Methods Used in Lobster and Crab Fishing" (Marine Laboratory, Aberdeen, Scotland).

[10] *See* page 49.

to handle and make it possible to increase the number of traps which can be stored on board ship. This latter factor is of especial importance where exposed coasts are fished or when crews are engaged in cruises of several days' duration; the ability to ship all the gear, for instance, to move to sheltered waters, is important. Where traps are fished not singly but with several attached along a common ground rope, small traps may permit working bigger fleets since it must be possible to accommodate the whole of one fleet on board.

Because of the advantage of being able to stow a large number of traps a variety of collapsible types have been designed. So far, however, none of these has found general acceptance amongst fishermen, although further trial may be advisable.

Bait

There is a natural tendency to think that a larger quantity of bait will attract more lobsters and crabs. In experiments, carried out with Scottish creels and Cornish pots in Orkney, the catch of lobsters and crabs with half a salted mackerel per trap was not significantly less than when three times this amount was used. The respective catches were 56 lobsters for single baitings compared with 59 for triple baitings.

Summary of Suggestions

1. If available, use fresh fish for bait.
2. Use net covered creels, avoiding wooden parts in construction as far as convenient; for instance, by adopting iron hoops and casting the concrete into the creel so that it forms part of the base.
3. Use double-headed creels with the heads high rigged and located in the sides.
4. Line the lower half of the head inlet with fine mesh netting.

5. In fishing lobsters only, adopt a small creel; when working crabs, a somewhat larger creel.

6. For an all-purpose compromise creel, an internal diameter of 5¼″ is suggested for the inner ring of the head, which should be fitted with a non-escape shutter. The latter should be regularly checked to ensure free action.

7. A smaller open eye (4½″) is preferable for lobster fishing in sheltered waters with a moderately well fished stock and daily hauling.

8. A shuttered eye is recommended where hauling is irregular.

9. 5¼″ shuttered eye is indicated for lobster fishing on exposed coasts where the stock is not much exploited, and for mixed lobster and crab fishing.

10. 5½″ open eye is suitable for crab fishing where hauling is regular daily (a non-escape shutter should be fitted where lobsters are likely to be caught in any small number).

11. In shallow water, when lobster fishing from small boats, use single creels, siting each creel.

12. In deeper water such as fished from larger boats, and during winter and bad weather by small boats, use creels in a trawl. The number of creels per trawl should be matched to the local bottom conditions. On patchy and rough bottoms short trawls of up to 10 creels are best. On uniformly good and even bottoms longer trawls of up to 50 creels are suitable.

13. Adapt the methods to the prevailing conditions. There is no one style of fishing or gear which will prove the best under all circumstances. The gear should be chosen to suit the style of fishing (lobsters and/or crabs, size of boat, nature of the bottom, exposure, etc.). Within these broad limits, detail should be varied to suit the season and the prevailing weather conditions.[11]

---

[11] Thomas, *op. cit.*

III

Artificial Bait

One respected and successful lobsterman has stated:

"Summer or winter, if you put a lobster pot where there are some lobsters, you will catch them. Too many fishermen blame their lack of accuracy and instincts for fishing on bait, weather behavior and other conclusions of their own. A lobster is simple enough. But if the guy going after him is even simpler, he might as well give up."

Lobster bait is usually the offal remaining after fillets have been removed from edible fish, or waste from sardine canning. It is packed in open barrels at filleting plants. These plants are often in large fishing centers such as Gloucester, Rockland, or even Provincetown, so extensive trucking is necessary to bring the bait to the many small lobstering ports.

A competing buyer of fish waste is the large fishmeal industry which grinds and dries this waste into chicken feed. The fishmeal people are able to offer increasingly higher prices for fish scrap—and higher prices than lobstermen can pay. Fish scrap which cost $1.00 a bushel a few years ago now sells for as high as $1.60. Moreover, fish catches are irregular; big runs of herring, etc., are followed by lean catches. The fishmeal factories can handle large batches of scrap when it is available, but the lobsterman cannot handle such surplus (except by a troublesome packing in barrels between layers of salt, i.e. pickling).

A manufactured bait would make a lobsterman independent of vagaries of the fish supply. Three days without bait (which may happen whenever red fish or herring are not running) means three days lost to the lobsterman, and three days every now and then amount to a sizable lost time. A manufactured bait could be shipped to any seaport in advance of its use and stored for a reasonable time. There would be none of the uncertainty involved in finding a truck which will take stinking fish scraps aboard and carry them from Gloucester to some out-of-the-way harbor—with little chance of a return cargo.

Any manufactured lobster bait will be smelly. But it would in no way be as offensive as are barrels of fish scrap stored in the sun on a lobster wharf, waiting to be used. Lobstermen are limited to the sites they can use for a wharf due to the odor, and many convenient locations are closed to them—locations which could be used if a manufactured bait stored in sealed containers could be used. Similarly, fish wharves which now are repugnant to summer visitors, boating parties, etc., would become attractive if a manufactured bait were available instead of fish scrap. Any man who sails can name a dozen harbors which are avoided because they stink too much.

Fish scrap is not only smelly and costly, but the bones of the fish can cause painful infections. When a lobsterman jams a handful of brim (scrap from filleted fish) on a bait hook, the fish bones can pierce his hand. Many fishermen have to take several days off during a season to recover from the infections.

Lobstermen are accustomed to think that the cost of their bait is the price they pay per bushel. This is correct if the buyer is large enough to pay for a truckload delivered at his wharf (as with the cooperatives), but the small buyer must add the cost of his time in going and coming to the seller's plant. In some ports, it has been customary for several lobstermen to join together and each take a turn in fetching the bait, often a full day's work. This should be added to the cost, but usually it is not.

There are about eight thousand lobstermen in New England. They average perhaps seventy-five pots per man. Pots are usually baited daily with three pounds of fish scraps, and the pots are fished eight months in the year. This adds up to over a million pounds of bait used daily. It is a big industry.

LobLure

The making of a synthetic lobster bait consists of finding a chemical lure and impregnating it into a carrier, such as a fish-oil soap or sawdust or fishmeal. One long series of experiments was carried out by a corporation called "Lob-Lure." *Maine Coast Fisherman* covered the story in the May and June issue of 1959.

The idea of a manufactured lobster bait dates back to early in World War II when two yachtsmen of Hingham, Massachusetts, veterans of World War I, Dudley Baker and Osborne M. Curtis, awoke to the help lobstermen might give to the war effort. They realized that lobstermen, who put to sea nearly every day in the week, were in a position to supplement our Naval Intelligence. Lobstermen see the burnt wreckage floating ashore, the bodies drifting in, or the strange light out on a point. So these two men sold our Navy the idea of taking them on as civilian Navy intelligence men, and they organized the lobstermen from Eastport to Connecticut into an information reporting group.

This work involved meeting many of the top liners among the lobstermen, and of course, learning something about lobstering and its problems. Curtis was particularly impressed with the problem of lobster bait—its smell, its cost, its likelihood of causing infection, and its seasonal scarcity.

So Curtis set out to develop a manufactured bait. He took in with him his sailing partner, this author, and they embarked on what became a six-year attempt, before they gave up. LobLure was the name of the corporation they formed and was to be the name of the artificial lobster bait they hoped to produce.

LobLure's first step was based on the generally accepted fact that oily fish such as herring or menhaden make the best bait; hence it was a fair deduction that the fish oil was the lobster attractant. Cloth bags were made, filled with sand, and saturated with uncooked herring oil. They wouldn't fish, gave no indication at all of being attractive. Four years later, and much wiser, LobLure concluded that the reason for oily fish being better bait was not because the oil was so attractive, but because the oil waterproofed the fish so that its flesh continued for a longer time to give off something that the lobsters wanted.

Oil had a place in all LobLure baits. One intelligent fisherman of the type whose statements of fact were generally true, and not colored by guesses and old wives tales, had found on the beach a full can of sardines. It was a large oval can, and had been punctured. The oil in it was a dark color similar to 600W engine oil. He used it in a pot and it caught lobsters as no other bait before or after had done. ★ ★

In an effort to duplicate this bait, several cans of sardines packed in different oils were purchased. Each can was punctured with several holes so that it would be infected by airborne bacteria. The different oils in the cans were olive oil, soy bean oil, and peanut oil. In some of the cans, the oil was poured off and molasses substituted, to test a rumor that molasses mixed with salt herring would improve that bait. Lobstermen sometimes find a method of fishing which is better, but they often attribute the wrong reason for their success.

The cans were left at the warm back of a stove to incubate any bacteria. In the end, they showed little evidence of deterioration. (Might this have been due to the oil covering the sardines and excluding the air?)

The cans were fished in comparison with redfish and were about 50 per cent as effective. The molasses treated cans were even less good. It was judged that the incubation time had not been long enough. From these tests it seemed as if two things had been learned. First, that when fish is coated with oil its rate of decomposition is slowed. Second, that the slight amount of oil which escaped from these tins actually did fish, though not well, and that the amount of fish flesh which left the can must have been very slight except as sand fleas chewed away portions of it.

It is hard to see how the oil in a sardine can can fish effectively as it apparently did, and to understand how oil, which will immediately rise to the surface, can diffuse enough to attract a lobster. Apparently, a lob- ★ ★

ster has some extremely delicate sense which can detect ★ ★ fish oil as it rises to the surface several fathoms above him. Lobsters on the bottom have been observed to follow an oil slick on the surface.

Apparently oil will carry the attractant to a lobster provided the oil is of the right nature, and provided the fish has been incubated with the right bacteria and to the right degree.

The baits which were fished that spring were ground fish with which redfish oil had been mixed. The fish scrap was incubated through its own marine bacteria, and was grown in a large bottle whose neck was closed by sterile cotton to exclude air bacteria. It incubated several times faster than frozen mackerel, presumably because in frozen fish the natural marine bacteria had been sterilized by the freezing. Frozen mackerel treated with oil fished about 75 per cent as well as natural fish bait.

Net-covered cotton pads tied up in a roll and saturated with herring oil were tried next. The pads seemed to lose little of their oil, as quantities could be squeezed out after two days' fishing. One of them caught several lobsters, showing that oil alone carries some attractant for lobsters.

The next bait was composed of mackerel pellets to which 15 per cent water had been added. They were air-inoculated for twenty-nine hours, and 10 per cent redfish oil was added. They fished about 25 per cent as well as natural fish bait. At the end of three days, they showed little deterioration and the center of the bait was packed down into a hard, impermeable mass.

From the start, LobLure was hampered by the widely varying opinions of different lobstermen. Many of these opinions were correct as to what would or would not attract lobsters, but no fisherman had made actual tests. LobLure had to have actual recorded tests if they were to be financed as a commercial business. So a member of the corporation went out with lobstermen when each test pot was baited and again when it was hauled. An accurate record was kept, as had probably never been done before. Tests were made with a string of pots, each alternate pot carrying the test bait, the other pots baited with redfish as a standard for comparison.

The importance of such recorded tests cannot be overemphasized. An example was the hauling of a test pot having five large lobsters in it. The lobsterman was delighted, waved his hands around and yelled, "You've got it, boys, you've got it!" If LobLure had had only his opinion to go on, they would have been delighted too. But the record of that string of pots showed this haul was a fluke, and it had not *averaged* as well as redfish.

In going out with lobstermen, the LobLure experimenters learned about lobsters as few people, except professional lobstermen, could. In addition, they learned which beliefs about lobsters were probably true, and which ones were doubtful. (For example, they *tested* the widely held belief that a brick soaked in kerosene "will fish like a fool." It won't. It will fish, but only about 60 per cent as well as redfish.) They learned fishing habits from Cutler, Maine, down through Connecticut; some were very intelligent and a few were just "notions."

Fundamentally, the problem was to learn what lobster-attractive substances there are in dead fish. It did not sound too difficult. But what is chemically in a dead fish *now* is not what is in that same fish an hour from now, since decomposition is constantly changing the structure of the fish.

Two chemicals were found in quantity, acetic acid and ammonium compounds. The problem then was to soak these materials up in a carrier, and there would be your bait. For a carrier, many things were tried, from sawdust to fishmeal. It was found that fishmeal was the best carrier, but fishmeal alone would not catch lobsters, particularly if it was oily. If the oil was pressed out it was much better (it is hard to understand this contradiction), and if only a little freshly ground fish were added it was very much better.

The next problem was how to dispense this bait in a

lobster pot. Three variables appeared which were not controllable:

1. The speed with which a bait dissolves is governed by where the pot lands on the ocean floor. If it lands in a valley through which tides and ocean currents sweep, the bait does not last long. If it lands in a placid spot, the bait does not dissolve quickly enough.

2. The temperature of the water also governs the speed. Warm summer water naturally dissolves a bait quicker than cold water. (Eventually, LobLure put out a different bait for winter fishing, when the water would be colder and the pots not hauled every day.)

3. The feeding cycle of lobsters, particularly before and after shedding, varies.

The most attractive method of dispensing a bait was to make it into a cake of salt-water soap, using fish oil as the necessary fat. It looked thoroughly commercial, easy to make and ship. But it had many disadvantages: either the soap was too soft and washed away quickly, or if it was harder, it did not fish well the first few days and finally did not fish at all, becoming a hard mass with a water-impervious shell. Notice how these experiments led toward a bait intended to fish for several days, instead of a one-day set. It was not a bad trend, as a bait which was good for several days could be sold for a higher price and be more profitable.

At this time, LobLure made its only experiments using ammonium compounds in the soap. They showed no indication of being attractants and were discontinued.

Many other materials were tried, such as coco butter. LobLure was encouraged to use this material because of a wreck *(The City of Salisbury)* near Graves Light in Boston Harbor. A steamer had piled up on an uncharted rock, and in its cargo were many cases of coco butter. A year later, a lobsterman had found that lobsters were thick around the submerged hull. It looked as though the coco butter might have attracted them, but the big supply of lobsters was probably due to the fact that this area had not been fished, rather than to the coco butter. Or it may be that the wreck played host to algae or shellfish attractive to lobsters. A salt-water angler knows that the most fish are found around wrecks. In any case, LobLure was not able to find any improved attraction from the use of coco butter. It is interesting to note that coco oil has the unusual property of blending with sea water.

The high content of phosphorus in lobster meat[1] led to a search to learn if phosphorus added to a bait could be an attractant. A Danish patent (No. 23445 of September 1918) was discovered and translated. It describes the use of phosphorus mixed with animal intestines in fish oil and claims it is a successful bait. (It does not specify lobsters.) Since there are two kinds of phosphorus, red and white, and since white phosphorus is highly poisonous and has to be kept under water lest it burst into flames, it seemed evident that red phosphorus was the only material to use.

Phosphorus, in either form, is insoluble in water. Hence its addition to a bait did not promise much. If the Danish patent had said phosphoric acid, it is possible that beneficial results might have been obtained, but that is not what the patent says.

The Danish formula was copied exactly and fished 22 times against redfish bait. None of the phosphorus baits caught even a single lobster, while the redfish baits caught 36 lobsters.

The next step was away from the soap cake into a paste bait. Since a soft bait would have to be held in a container, as well as need more protection from fish and sea fleas, it was necessary to develop something better than the old-style wooden bait box. Over fifty models were built and tried. Eventually, LobLure settled on a cylindrical screen container (2″ diameter x 8″) made of heavy wire with wooden bungs for ends and lined with plastic window screening to exclude sea fleas. With the containers went an ice cream scoop to handle the pasty bait. With the paste baits a new formula was evolved which included some ground fresh fish scrap, and had good fishing qualities.

---

[1] *See* page 28.

The use of ground fish as a part of LobLure was based on the fact that fish in bulk, such as the carcass of a filleted fish, presents only part of its surface to the sea water. When this same carcass is ground up, the areas presented to the sea water are greatly increased. LobLure found that two ounces of ground fish could be as attractive to lobsters as several pounds of unground fish. As always, LobLure fetched up against a new problem, namely that the ground fish would become compacted so hard that water could not enter to dissolve the bait. They had to have an open bait or a bait whose binder would dissolve and let the water in. That meant a bait needing careful protection and control. The control was an important feature, and actually meant that LobLure had to sell a *method of fishing* rather than just a bait.

The amount of the catch was not dependable. Sometimes the bait was twice as good as redfish, but more often the catch would be only 60 per cent as good. Several of the fishermen would not believe that two lots of bait were the same formula. They *were* the same, and were very carefully watched to prevent any variation. That they did not fish equally was due to the many uncontrollable factors involved. For instance, the water content as well as the chemical nature of fish scrap would vary with its age, and it was not possible to buy this scrap at a definite number of hours old. Then again, the oiliness of the scrap would vary depending on the kind of fish being filleted. In addition, the use of fresh fish scrap increased the cost. LobLure was actually trending back towards the selling of brim as a manufactured bait.

Many other chemicals were tried, covering a wide range such as butyric acid, propionic acid, amino compounds, and tri-methylamine of awful odor, but with no spectacular results.

LobLure ended up convinced that any successful bait must be on the acid side. This conclusion eliminated the use of salt-water soap as a dissolving binder, as any soap would be an alkaline.

LobLure also found that any bait using a fish oil must *not* be a cooked bait, since cooking turned the oil into a water impenetrable varnish.

And then, all its capital gone, LobLure went out of business in 1949. Why? Two opinions are quoted: "We can only surmise that the reason that LobLure does not consistently fish as well, or better than, redfish or other fish bait, is because it is lacking in a concentration of materials which are most attractive to lobsters. . . . . LobLure failed because it concentrated on one type of lure. It had several possible paths of development open, but followed one path in great detail without first exploring other paths to learn which was most promising." And the path it chose was not good enough: six years of work, over $30,000 spent, 4,000 supervised tests made of some 350 formulas, and no commercial results.

Freon Gas

Some interesting experiments with artificial bait were made by Dr. Harry Lee, formerly of Stonington, Maine. He used freon gas mixed with fish oil, in a container which liberated the gas slowly.

His idea was based on the fact that freon gas will absorb the oil (and the attendant odor). This gas also dissolves in sea water so that the oil carried by the gas would be dissipated in the water. Its effect was not to liberate globules of oil (which would immediately rise to the surface), but to spread the oil throughout the water.

Result: "It would catch lobsters, but not so well as any number of baits used around Stonington."

Light for Lures

It seemed as though light might attract lobsters.

Lobstermen claim that they cannot catch lobsters ★ ★ during periods of high-course tides. This is when the moon is full and brightest. Some fishermen attribute this to the brightness of the moonlight, but this does not seem to be the answer, as poor fishing occurs during high tides even when the moon is obscured. ★★

Recently, during a five-year period, one investigator tried every combination of lights that he could devise. Here are some of the schemes:

First, he worked largely with real radium salts such as are painted on watch dials; also Willemite, a zinc material which glows brilliant green under the influence of radium radiations. Another chemical tested was a phosphorus compound and zinc cadmium sulphite. His best mounting of radium was inside the ball-like glass top of a coffee percolator. This glass could be plugged with a rubber cork, making it watertight (see Figure 15). This device was tried in various degrees of brightness because it was feared that the light might be too bright for the light-sensitive eyes of a lobster in twenty fathoms of water, where there is normally almost no light. Tests were attempted in the usual lobster tanks in a very dark room, at first, but this investigator had no confidence in them since he knew, as do lobstermen, that lobsters act very differently in a tank than they do on the ocean floor. All tests thereafter were made in pots under actual fishing conditions, and a careful record was kept.

Fig. 15

Several skin-diving photographers have reported that sea water absorbs red light rays completely at 30 feet deep—as it also does yellow and orange—in fact, at over 90 feet deep, all things become a monotonous blue-grey. Artificial light, however, shows up all the true colors, hence those highly colored photographs taken with flash bulbs.

Many tests were made, covering the glass knob with different colored cellophane. Cellophane was used because it would not disintegrate in water, and because different colors of cellophane had widely varying properties of filtering out either ultra-violet or infra-red rays. These lures were tried in different positions in the pot, and were mounted to be either stationary or moving. Some even had plastic fins attached so that ocean currents would make them rock back and forth to produce a flickering light. None of these tests produced a lure anywhere near as good as redfish.

Next, mirrors were tried. This scheme had been tried by LobLure, too, using a weighted, wedge-shaped wooden block on two faces of which small hand mirrors were mounted. The wedge shape was used to deflect the light rays coming down from above the water so they would shoot off parallel to the ocean floor (the angle of incidence being equal to the angle of deflection). This device had been successful *once* (three counters in one pot) but it had not worked at all since then. Nor did it with these new tests, and it could only be concluded that its one-time success was a fluke. Every lobsterman knows that under some conditions of hunger or curiosity a lobster will enter an unbaited pot.

Another experiment with mirrors was to put one-half a teaspoonful of mercury in a small square glass bottle, using just enough mercury so that the bottle would almost float and, therefore, be moved by a very slight ocean current. This bottle, hung in a pot, would rock back and forth slowly flickering its reflected light. The idea was that a flickering light is more attention getting than a stationary light (notice any flickering advertising sign).

Another trial using the mirror idea was to coat the inside of a glass bottle with herring-scale lacquer, the hope being that herring scale, a natural reflector of the ocean, might flash a light more acceptable to a lobster. It proved nothing.

A resident of Damariscotta came up with a scheme which sounded encouraging. He used the principle of the Geissler tube, which some of us remember from high school physics. He had made a sealed glass globe, about three inches in diameter, containing neon gas and about a teaspoon of mercury. When the globe was shaken, the movement of the mercury generated static electricity, and the electricity lit up the neon gas just as a neon sign is lit up by current electricity. It gave a flash of orange light.

These globes were held in string bait bags and hung in the pot. They were fished in South Bristol, and they caught lobster equally as well as fish bait. (The fishing was poor for either the lights or the bait, but the results were almost the same.) It seemed to prove that light would attract lobsters, but it was not practical. The tests were made in relatively shallow water near a reef where there was great turbulence to shake up the globes. In deeper water, where there is little turbulence, they were not agitated enough and would not light up.

Fig. 16. The sealed glass globe

A number of the globes were made by a glass blower. They contained different gases and varying amounts of mercury, in the hope that some combination might be found that would light up with little movement; but they were not successful.

In desperation, the investigator hunted for some means other than ocean currents to shake the glass. In a tank test, he tried attaching the snout of a lobster (which would be left in the pot) by a cord to the globe. When the lobster jerked violently backward it would produce a tiny flash in the globe. In a pot, the light did not prove to be bright enough to attract a lobster; and the lobster proved to tire quickly of his backward jerking and became quiet.

Pursuing the idea of reflected light, our man next experimented with a wide variety of sheet plastic vanes to be hung in pots. These were white, usually twisted in a shallow spiral, and mounted with swivels to rotate in ocean currents. Others were coated with different colors of luminous paints such as used on lobster pot buoys. None of them was effective.

The next experiments were made with an electric light mounted inside of a Mason jar. The thought behind these trials was that there might be some rays in the radium-salt lights which were repellent to lobsters. An electric light might not have such repellent rays. A tiny bulb was used, of the sort used by doctors to examine the inner ear. It was connected to flashlight batteries, and would burn for several days. It also was ineffective.

Maine Coast Fisherman, in June 1956, carried an article by an Orrs Island lobsterman describing his success in using white coffee mugs as his only bait. This did not seem possible in view of the many light-reflecting tests which had been made. But, so as not to overlook any bets, a dozen mugs were tested—and they caught nothing.

To try a diffused instead of a concentrated light, a silvered Christmas tree ball was hung in a pot. The spherical surface reflected light in all directions from its upper hemisphere. Also, and for the same purpose, white glass marbles were placed in the glass percolator tops. The radium salt was applied to the small end of the rubber cork. Thus, the light was reflected as diffused light by the marble rather than striking directly into the water. No success.

As a last shot, a number of the above tests were repeated, using bait as well as the light. If the light and bait *together* fished better than bait alone, then one could be sure that the light was helpful. In most trials the combination caught fewer lobsters than bait alone. The best he could do was to occasionally have the combination fish as well as bait alone. These last tests were made with a lighted percolator top secured in the small end of a sheet rubber cone. The cone was mounted over the bait so that its light shone on the bait, but the light source itself was invisible to a lobster.

There have been articles in newspapers telling of fish lures which attracted through sound. To try out this idea, and purely as a shot in the dark, a loud ticking Ingersoll watch was placed in a Mason jar and hung in a pot—with no results except that the jar leaked in the first test and the watch was ruined.

There are still several entirely different approaches to the problem of attracting lobsters. But they take time and are often expensive.

A word of caution: be very careful how you play with radium salts. They can and do cause cancer if improperly handled. The girls who paint watch dials work behind glass shields and are frequently checked by health officials.

This history ends with no practical lure. It is valuable in that it provides a starting point for further development, and it should save needless duplicating of experiments already made. Knowledge of what not to do is often valuable.

In the history of this country, if a need is great enough, someone has always fulfilled that need. The need for a manufactured lobster bait is great. Someone will find the answer.

IV

Artificial Sea Water for Inland Tanks[1]

The need for artificial sea water stems from inland restaurants and fish dealers desiring to stock and exhibit *live* lobsters. Today, lobsters are a luxury food, and if they cannot be shown as alive much of their appeal is lost.

It would be of enormous gain to the lobster industry if the keeping of live lobsters away from the sea should become more commonplace. The scope of the market would be tremendously increased, and would be less a matter of feast or famine than it is today. Wherever there is competition for an article of limited supply, the price rises. Think of what this could mean to lobstermen.

The use of artificial sea water is well known, and it is practiced by several successful lobster dealers. It can preserve lobsters just as well as natural sea water, if *all* the requirements are met.

> In order to create the best possible storage conditions for live lobster, it is suggested first of all to look at its natural habitat. The lobster lives in salt water and can only stand a relatively small change in the salt concentration of the water. A concentration of about 25 per 1000 salt or more seems to be necessary for the lobster's well-being.
>
> The greater part of the year the lobster lives at low temperatures (41°F.-50°F.) and it only seeks warmer water (approximately 60°F.) in the short spawning period. As the lobster eats sparsely in the cold period of the year, it is difficult to lure it into the lobster traps during this time.
>
> Although the lobster requires an almost constant salt concentration in the water, it is capable of getting

---

[1] Research Bulletin No. 11 (1953) by John S. Getchell of Sea and Shore Fisheries is devoted to this subject. Another bulletin, "Storage of Live Lobsters," by F. Bramsnaes and Jan Boetius, was published in 1953 by the Physiological Laboratory, Charlottenlund, Denmark. Its studies were made with the English lobster, which is almost identical with the lobster of New England and Canada.

along well within a wide range of temperatures, that is, from a few degrees up to approximately 77°F. A continuous supply of fresh oxygenous water is, however, essential. As will be seen from the following, this involves a number of technical difficulties for the fish dealer, especially in warm weather. . . .

Salt is essential to the lobster's functions, which is why the salt concentration in the lobster's blood has to be constant. In sea water, the salt concentration in the lobster's blood is approximately the same as that of the surrounding water. If the sea water is diluted, for instance by adding fresh water, the salts will be washed out of the lobster's blood into the water. The lobster is not capable of retaining the normal and necessary concentration of salt in the blood.

Experiments carried out with various mixtures of fresh water and sea water showed that the animals became very feeble when the salt concentration in the water was low (from 25 per 1000 salt down to 20 per 1000). Under such conditions, the rate of metabolism (oxygen consumption) increased about 50 per cent, which entails, as will be seen later on, another technical difficulty in connection with the storage of lobster. At even lower salt concentrations (from 20 per 1000 and downwards), the lobster could only remain alive for a very short time. . . . .

The word " salt " as used in the foregoing should be understood to be the mixture of mineral salts usually present in sea water. This mixture contains apart from ordinary salt (by technicians called sodium chloride, ordinarily called kitchen salt or just common salt), also numerous other kinds of salts, which are all more or less vital to the growth of the lobster. Many of these salts only appear in very small quantities in sea water.

The mixture of artificial sea water which was used in these experiments contains five of the most important components of natural sea water approximately in the same concentration as in sea water. There exist various recipes for such artificial sea water. In these experiments, two of these were examined, i.e., the mixture of van Deurs and a mixture by Schmaltz. Although both mixtures have been found satisfactory, the one by Schmaltz is recommended, chiefly because this mixture comes a bit closer to the composition of natural sea water than that of van Deurs. The Schmaltz recipe is as follows:

Sodium chloride ($NaCl$)	14.52 lbs.
Magnesium sulphate ($MgSo_4,7H_2O$)	3.52 lbs.
Magnesium chloride ($MgCl_2,6H_2O$)	2.86 lbs.
Calcium chloride ($CaCl_2,2H_2O$)	.7 lb.
Potassium chloride (KCl)	.33 lb.
Total approximately	22 lbs.

The specified amounts of salt are mixed with 92 gallons ordinary drinking water [check to see that it has not been chlorinated]. It is necessary to stir the solution at regular intervals until all the salt has been dissolved. This process takes about two hours. The various salts can be obtained from chemical firms and be used successfully, although they often cause some turbidity in the solution as some of the substances may not be water soluble. . . . .

All the salts, with the exception of potassium chloride, can be stored for a considerable length of time, even when mixed, provided they are kept in a dry place. Potassium chloride is highly water absorbent and even in ordinary air very soon liquifies. It is therefore suggested to buy this salt immediately before use and take out only the amount needed for one mixture unless it is kept in a tightly closed glass jar.

Apart from experiments with the above mentioned two recipes, experiments have also been carried out with plain water to which was added various kinds of ordinary salts, mainly because these ordinary salts have been used commercially in storage water with little or no success. In these experiments, the salt concentration of the water was about 30 per 1000. It was established that ordinary salt (kitchen salt) had a fatal effect on the lobster even after only a few hours' storage in the water. The reason for this is the lack of the other mineral salts mentioned in the recipe.

Other products are commercially sold under trade names and have been examined. It is true that these salts have all been extracted from natural sea water by evaporation, but since the various kinds of salt do not crystallize to the same extent, the salt mixture often varies and is very far from the composition of natural sea water. Analyses also show considerable differences in the composition of the mentioned salts. It should be noted as an important fact that the calcium content of all the mentioned products is small. Although this component is only found in relatively small quantities in natural sea water, it is absolutely essential to the lobster.[2]

The Sea and Shore Fisheries bulletin gives three formulas for artificial sea water. These formulas are more complicated, but they come from *The Oceans, The Chemistry and Biology of Sea Water* by Sverdrup et al, and should be superior.

Experiments have also proved that artificial sea water seems to be quite as useful as natural sea water. Lobsters have easily been able to remain alive in both kinds of water for months.

It has been maintained that the lobster once removed from a storage tank containing artificial sea water quickly becomes weak and limp; this has led to a further examination of lobsters which had been stored in artificial sea water for about two weeks. After being removed from the tank, they were kept in cold, moist air at about 50°F. They remained so for almost two

---

[2] Bramsnaes and Boetius, *op. cit.*

weeks in apparent good condition and were then transferred to the storage tank undamaged. . . . .

So far, it has not been possible to point out why the lobsters became weak when removed from the storage tank as described in the experiment.

The question of how often to change the artificial sea water depends primarily upon the type of tank used. . . . . Like most living animals, the lobster is dependent on the oxygen in the air in order to breathe. In its natural habitat, the lobster utilizes the oxygen which is found in liberal amounts in fresh sea water.

When sea water contains as much oxygen as can possibly be dissolved in it, it is " saturated." The amount of oxygen dissolved in sea water depends on the temperature of the water; the warmer the water, the less oxygen it contains.

Thus, one of the greatest problems of storing live lobsters in tanks on land for commercial purposes is the necessity of producing the required supply of oxygen. Because of limited space, the water content of the tank is necessarily small in comparison to the number of lobsters stored, which very soon consume the supply of oxygen on hand. If the water was not constantly supplied with fresh oxygen, the lobsters would simply choke to death. During the experiments, it has been found that the lobsters became " lifeless " when the oxygen content of the water went below approximately ¼ of the oxygen content of saturated water. If this " lifeless " condition has already set in, it is essential for the lobster, in order to survive, to be supplied with fresh water within an hour or two. The technical requirements of the storage tank are mainly based on the necessity of a constant supply of oxygen. It should be noted that if the supply of oxygen should fail (for instance, in case of a motor stop), it is most important to make sure that the tank containing the lobsters is quickly emptied. In case of a motor stop, the drainage system should automatically start. . . . .

The next experiments were carried out to determine the oxygen consumption of the lobster at various temperatures. Within the examined ranges of temperature (35°F. to 86°F.), it was found that the lobster's oxygen consumption was more than doubled if the temperature was raised 50°F.

Experiments also showed that the lobster's oxygen consumption did not change whether the animal was placed under an intense light or in total darkness.

However, if the salt concentration of the water was reduced to under 25 per 1000, for instance by adding fresh water, the lobster's oxygen consumption was increased considerably.

When the lobster was fed with the meat of a herring, the oxygen consumption was almost doubled. This increase in the oxygen consumption rate was still noticeable on the third day after the feeding. This experiment, as well as the two preceding ones, was carried out at 60°F.

These experiments also showed that small lobsters (about ¾-pound) have a higher oxygen consumption than larger lobsters (2 to 4 pounds). It was also found that the oxygen consumption of a great number of lobsters stored together was somewhat lower per pound per hour than that of a single lobster.

The influence of temperature on the growth of lobsters stored in reservoirs on land. With a view to finding the most economical way of storing lobsters, it is important that the oxygen consumption rate of the lobster be kept as low as possible. The lower the consumption of oxygen, the less water circulation (fresh oxygen supply) is required in the tank. A low oxygen consumption rate also ensures that the waste matter within a certain storage period is small, that is, the nutritious condition is not reduced a great deal. The following conclusions may be drawn from the above-mentioned experiments: by lowering the temperature, the rate of oxygen consumption is reduced very effectively. By refrigerating the storage water, many advantages are gained which can best be seen by comparing the storage conditions in a tank with a temperature of about 60°F. (approximately the temperature of the surrounding air) and those in a refrigerated storage tank (about 42°F.).

Pollution. In an indoor, not refrigerated, storage tank, the temperature stays around 60°F. most of the time, though it may go higher, especially in the middle of the lobster season where the demand for storage is at its peak. At 60°F., the lobsters' oxygen consumption rate is quite high, and the oxygen solubility of the water is correspondingly low, which is why the oxygen supply of the storage water is soon used up. A third disadvantage of this high temperature is that the lobsters' oxygen consumption results in an increased production of dung. The water soon becomes polluted, malodorous; mucus and foam appear on the surface of the water. These conditions seem, however, only to have a slight poisonous effect on the lobster. This problem has been discussed extensively among specialists in this field and thorough experiments have shown that as long as the oxygen supply is sufficient, the animals can live for months in relatively strong pollutions of their own dung. It has also been important to ascertain whether the flavor of the lobsters' meat would be affected by the polluted water. Therefore, a number of persons were served both freshly caught lobsters and lobsters which had been stored for a long period of time, and they were unable to detect any difference in taste. It was found that lobsters stored up to a month in quite strong pollutions of dung had the same taste as that of freshly caught lobsters. However, the immediate impression of the hygienic conditions in such a tank is not exactly inspiring. The greatest disadvantage is that the dung also consumes large amounts of oxygen. Consequently, this requires special methods for oxygen supply as well as filters and a strong water circulation. It has been found that the dung products of a one-pound lobster stored for about a week in 26 quarts of sea water (which was not changed during the week) at a temperature of 60°F. consumes approximately almost three times as much as the oxygen consumption of the lobster itself.

When the lobster has lived for some time at a high temperature (60°F.-68°F.), its quality deteriorates. Experiments have proved, however that—strangely enough—there is almost no weight reduction in lobsters stored up to two months. . . . .

After a long period of storage, it has been experienced that the texture of the meat has a tendency to change—it becomes more "filamentous" [stringy]. It has been discussed if it was more advantageous to feed the animals in order to avoid this deterioration of texture; feeding can take place, as the lobsters are quite willing to eat at high temperature. At low temperature (for instance, 41°F.), they refuse to eat. It is, however, rather difficult to distribute the food evenly in a tank containing a large amount of lobsters and the water may become polluted in doing so. From the abovementioned experiments, the following conclusions can be drawn: the oxygen consumption of a well-fed lobster is doubled compared to that of an unfed lobster stored at the same temperature. The amount of dung products, which more or less equals the consumption of oxygen, is estimated to be doubled, i.e., the oxygen consumption of the whole system (lobster plus water) is doubled. In addition, the left-over food also consumes oxygen. It is, of course, impossible to give a definite figure, but it is estimated to be quite high, judging by the way the lobsters devour their food. When lobsters are being fed with the meat of a herring, they tear it to shreds which almost form a cloud around the eating animals causing putrefaction to set in. It is, therefore, advisable not to feed the lobsters because of the very heavy demand on the oxygen supply of the storage water.

Experiments have shown that a lobster can do without food for more than three months at 60°F. Because of the already mentioned deterioration of the meat texture, it is recommended that the lobsters should not be stored for more than three or four weeks under such conditions.

Finally, it can be mentioned that the lobsters show great activity at high temperature and may easily harm each other. If the animals appear dull at high temperature, the reason is probably lack of sufficient oxygen.[3]

Sea and Shore Fisheries has undertaken to determine the best temperature of water in which lobsters should be kept. They used four temperature ranges, namely: 35°-40°F.; 45°-50°F.; 55°-60°F.; and 65°-70°F.

The activity of the lobsters was observed in each range for five days, and from the results a temperature was chosen at which the water was kept throughout the study. Thirty fresh lobsters were used in each temperature range. The results obtained were as follows:

Temperature Range	*Activity*	*Remarks*
35°-40°F.	Very sluggish	No mortality at 5 days
45°-50°F.	Moderately active	No mortality at 5 days
55°-60°F.-	Active to sluggish	10 dead at 5 days; all sluggish after 3 days
65°-70°F.	Active to sluggish	20 dead after 24 hours; all dead after 48 hours

From the results obtained, the 45°-50°F. range was chosen as the highest temperature to be used.

[3] Bramsnaes and Boetius, *op. cit.*

This choice of temperature seems to have been chosen because the lobsters were noticeably active. It is lower than the 60°F. used in the Danish experiments, but it is to be questioned if an even lower temperature (40°-45°F.) might not be even more effective. The lobsters would eat less, they would move about less, they are less scrappy, and there would be less dung, all of which would reduce the all-important oxygen consumption. One objection seems to be that they are very sluggish in colder water. But since a lobster regains his activity when he is taken from the water (as when a lobster is exhibited to a buyer), its sluggishness in the water seems a small matter. Another objection is that 48°F. is approximately the temperature of the lobster as unpacked from an iced shipping container. Lobsters react strongly to too abrupt changes in temperature. It is possible to kill a lobster by increasing the temperature too quickly. On the other hand, they react less strongly to a decrease in temperature.

As far as can be seen, the "warm" storage has no natural advantage for the lobster. The following is a short summary of the disadvantages:

1. The oxygen solubility of the warmer water is small.
2. The oxygen consumption of the lobsters is fairly large.
3. The amount of dung is proportionately large and the decrease of oxygen in the water becomes even larger.
4. By storing the lobster over a longer period, the texture of the meat deteriorates. Feeding is no help as it causes a still larger decrease in the oxygen supply of the tank.
5. The great activity of the lobsters is a disadvantage.

Storage conditions at a low temperature (42°F.). The five disadvantages found under "warm" storage conditions can all be avoided when the temperature is lowered:

1. The colder water dissolves more oxygen.

2. At 42°F. the lobster's oxygen consumption rate is half the rate of that at 60°F.

3. As the amount of dung products is reduced, the consumption of oxygen is also lowered.

4. The deterioration of texture is insignificant, even when the lobsters have been stored from two to three months. Feeding is no problem as the animals do not eat at low temperatures.

5. The activity of the animals is low—they do not harm each other and are easy to handle. It is desirable that the lobsters for sale show a certain amount of vitality and it should be noted that the cold as well as the "dull" animals become lively when removed from the tank.[4]

Supply of oxygen. The Maine experiments used two ½" aerated nozzles per lobster tank. Additional aeration by compressed air was found unnecessary as long as the recirculation system was in operation.

As mentioned in the description of the experiments, the necessary oxygen supply is of the greatest importance. The oxygen in the storage water is replenished when the oxygen of the air is forced down into the water. This may be done by means of a pump which continually sucks the water from the bottom of the tank, then forces it through a sprayer and down into the water again. When the water falls from the sprayer down into the water, it is replenished with oxygen in the air. Especially when the water breaks through the surface, particles of air are forced down into the water, which absorbs the oxygen. When the surface is smooth, only small amounts of oxygen can penetrate it. It is, therefore, important to create the greatest possible movement of the water surface. In larger tanks, it is

[4] Bramsnaes and Boetius, *op. cit.*

often necessary to install several sprayers and the oxidation of the water becomes more effective when these are placed high above the tank. Other effective methods for oxidizing the water are, of course, possible.

The pump used for circulating the water must have a fixed capacity depending primarily on the number of lobsters stored and on the temperature of the water. The table below indicates the approximate capacities of the pumps; at high storage temperatures (60°F. or more), these figures may deviate. It is assumed that the entire surface is put in motion by the pumps. [5]

Temperature		*Pounds lobster in the tank*			
°F.		*55*	*110*	*220*	*660*
41	Quarts pumped:	127	254	530	1690
50		210	429	980	2970
59		357	742	1590	4870

Maine tanks held 300 gallons and 50 pounds of lobsters. The pump circulated 400 gallons per hour.

Foaming was a problem encountered by Maine after the lobsters had been in the tank three days, and it lasted from seven to twelve days. This foam was formed as the water was discharged into the lobster tank in a soap-sudsy mass and spread across the surface of the water in the tank.

To combat this problem, "Antifoam A," a silicone defoamer, was employed and found very effective at a concentration of ten parts per million in dispersing the foam. This material had no apparent adverse effect upon the lobsters at this concentration.

According to the Danish bulletin, "The water should be changed as soon as it becomes dark, muddy and malodorous in spite of constant filtration. As long as the water stays clear without much foam formation, it can be used. Normally, a change is only needed once or twice during the lob-

[5] Bramsnaes and Boetius, *op. cit.*

ster season, depending on the prevailing temperatures—the cooler the water, the longer the lobsters will keep." This is more often than the once a year Maine recommends, but these Danish experiments circulated much less water.

Filtration is an important part of processing artificial sea water. It was considered essential to the commercial lobster aquariums which have been promoted. Removal of fish dung is believed to be very important in goldfish tanks, and perhaps salt water snails in a lobster aquarium would clean the water as they are supposed to do in goldfish tanks.

Yet the Danish experiments clearly show that strong pollutions of dung do not affect the lobsters so long as enough oxygen is present. In contradiction, it is believed by many lobster dealers that the dung of lobsters can kill other lobsters lying in the lower layers in a shipping container. This is a reason for keeping freshly caught lobsters in a tank for at least one day so that their bowels may be emptied.

Dr. Thomas in his "Lobster Storage" says:

> When lobsters have been in air, as when travelling, the dung builds up inside of them. In summer this accumulation may be considerable. The dung will be thrown off when the lobsters are put into water. In consequence, if possible, lobsters should not be put into re-circulating water after travelling but first given an hour or so in fresh sea water. (Such treatment is hardly possible in inland installations.) A weak lobster stands a better chance of survival if it is lowered slowly into the water tail first so that the water can flood gently through the gill chamber, thereby avoiding air locks.[6]

Maine used a cloth filter of Lumite, a plastic cloth with 36 threads to the inch and a porosity of .008 inches. It did not filter out much of the suspended matter. Enough remained to give a slight turbidity to the water.

---

[6] Published by the Marine Laboratory, Aberdeen, Scotland.

Feeding. It has been shown that lobsters can do without food for more than three months at 60°F., and at low temperatures refuse to eat. Maine noted that for the first two or three days after lobsters were put into refrigerated artificial sea water, they would feed, but after that period they refused all food. They reported that the reason for this behavior was unknown. Perhaps the chilling of the lobsters and loss of appetite is a slower process than realized and the lowering of oxygen consumption is very gradual.

Acclimatization. The Canadian "Atlantic Biological Station Note No. 137," states: "Lobsters take longer to become acclimated than you might expect. If the salt content or the amount of dissolved oxygen is suddenly reduced, it takes the lobsters about a week to become acclimated. It takes even longer to acclimate to changing water temperatures. If, for example, lobsters are caught in deep, cool water (50°F.) and held in warm water (65°F.), they will not become fully acclimated to the warmer water for at least three weeks." A similar danger occurs when lobsters are taken from a refrigerated truck and plunged into the warmed summer water of a pound. Lobsters which have become warmed in transit (the baskets of caught lobsters in a fisherman's boat) should not be immediately plunged into very cold sea water. A shallow warmer pool as a vestibule to the main pound might be the answer.

The tank system. The tank is commonly made of wood, but concrete tanks will serve. After a concrete tank has been cast, it should be filled with a soda solution for several days. Then it should be emptied, rinsed well, and scrubbed.

It is essential to take care that the lobsters are not exposed to some poisonous materials. Certain metals—even in small amounts—have a dangerous effect. Copper and copper alloys, e.g. brass, must be completely avoided when the tank is built. Zinc and lead, galvanized materials, or materials containing lead are also poisonous and must, therefore, not come in contact with the lobsters or the storage water. Aluminum, iron, and rust are not harmful to the animals.

If the coils of the refrigeration unit are copper, they can be coated with plastic paint, but plastic is a poor conductor of heat. A black colored plastic is preferable to the semi-transparent variety, since the latter allows the growth of algae. Stainless steel is the best, but it should be free from copper. Some brands are not.

As to size, the general rule in Denmark is that 22 pounds of lobster require 26 to 40 gallons of storage water. The Maine recommendation is that 2 gallons of water be allowed for each pound of lobsters.

Every tank should have a drainage plug. Lobsters will not live long if their water ceases to circulate, but they will live in the air so long as the tissue of their lungs is kept moist, and they are cool enough (about two weeks). In case of failure of the circulating pump, the tank must be drained at once.

Summary

The Danish article sums up by stating that the correct "artificial sea water can fully replace natural sea water."

The conclusions of the Maine tests are:

1. That lobsters were able to live in recirculated natural sea water for a period of seven days without any appreciable mortality, and for fourteen days with very little mortality.

2. That with the addition of fresh lobsters this cycle could be repeated using the same water for a year's time, provided that the specific gravity was kept constant.

3. That artificial sea water compared very favorably with natural sea water under the conditions of the experiment.

4. That within the limits already stated, it is feasible to handle lobsters commercially in such a system.

Notice that an artificial sea water solution being the equal of actual sea water does not mean that lobsters will not die in such captivity; they will and they do in tanks supplied with plenty of fresh sea water.

The following graph from Sea and Shore Fisheries Bulletin 11 shows the death rate in fresh natural sea water. No lobsters died in the first seven days. But thereafter the death rate rose somewhat until after twelve days the mortality sharply increased. All fifty lobsters in the test were dead in thirty-two days. The water was cooled to 45°-50°F.

The bulletin of Sea and Shore Fisheries (1960) "The Storage of Live Lobsters in Recirculated-Refrigerated Tanks," by Phillip L. Goggins, corroborates many of the facts given above. Its formula for artificial sea water is the same

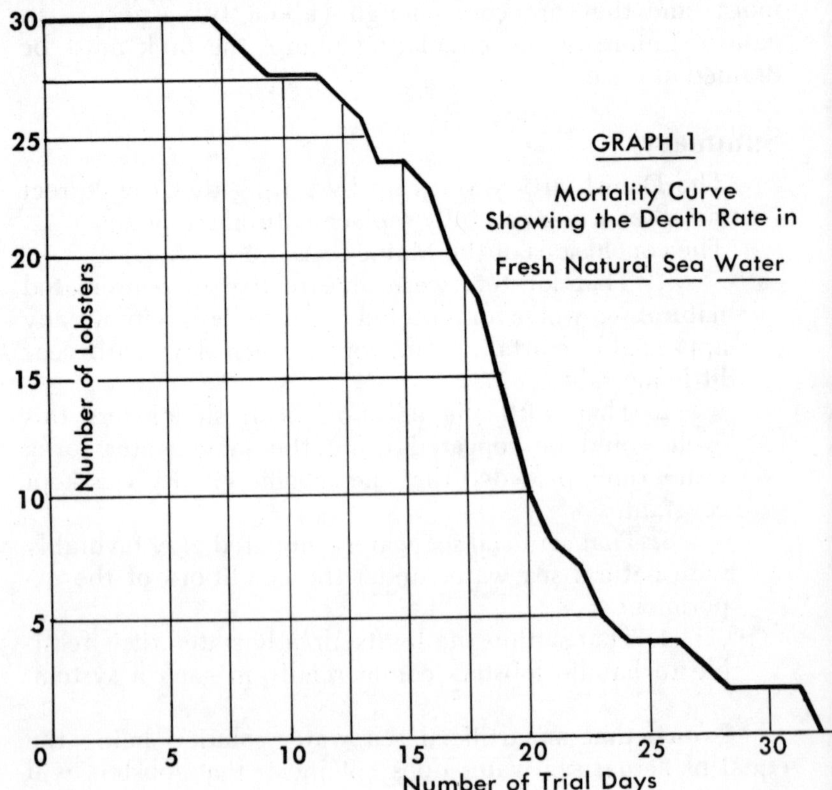

as the one given here. In addition, this bulletin gives this information:

> The optimum for salinity for lobsters is from 2.9 to 3.5%. The salinity of the Schmaltz formula is 3.4 per cent. Before placing lobsters in the solution, check with your local water department to see whether there is any residual chlorine in the water. Chlorine is toxic to lobsters at .1 part per million. This can be corrected, if it exists, by passing the water through an activated charcoal filter or by recirculating the water for two hours.
>
> Only vigorous lobsters should be stored in recirculated systems. Generally, it is not difficult to obtain such lobsters during the cold months. However, during the period of July through October, one cannot depend upon receiving vigorous lobsters. During this period many of the lobsters have recently passed through the enervating moulting process. Furthermore, they are much more likely to have been exposed to adverse conditions of crowding and high temperatures during the pre-shipment storage. They should be carefully graded with only the most lively-appearing chosen for shipment. They should be packed and handled as carefully as if they were eggs.
>
> Even with such care during the July to October period, loss will sometimes occur, but without careful treatment during this period, serious loss is almost certain to occur. Therefore, it is essential to find a firm which specializes in supplying lobsters to recirculating systems. There are several in Maine. The names of these can be obtained from the Department of Sea and Shore Fisheries.

The excellent "do's" and "don'ts" from this bulletin follow:

Symptoms and Probable Causes of Death of Lobsters in Recirculated Holding Systems

Symptoms	*Probable Cause*	*Correction*
Lobster becomes increasingly weak and sluggish; dies in spread-eagle position.	1. Lack of oxygen 2. Copper poisoning 3. Poisoning due to breakdown of waste material	1. Remove some lobsters from system or increase circulation. 2. Remove copper from system. 3. Change water.
Many dead upon arrival. Show above symptoms when placed in water. More active lobsters, upon removal from water, die in 15-20 minutes. If wounded, bleed to death quickly.	Bacterial Disease, Gaffkyaremia	1. Salvage weak lobsters. 2. Notify Sea and Shore Fisheries.
Lobsters become increasingly weak and sluggish. Die in spread-eagle position with bloating, while still alive, at junctions of carapace and tail, and at junction of walking legs and body.	1. Fresh water 2. Acute Gas Disease	1. Check salinity and correct. 2. Check vacuum side of pump for possible air leaks and correct.
Lobster may show mild irritation (more activity than normal) walk on tips of walking legs with tail angled upward, then lose sense of balance, fall on side or back, unable to right itself. May not die for week or more.	1. Mild Gas Disease 2. Mild insecticide poisoning	1. Same as #2 above. 2. Drain tank thoroughly. Clean with strong alkali. Replace water.
Lobsters hyperactive. May leap out of water. May die in 2-4 hours.	Acute insecticide poisoning	Same as #2 above.
Lobsters hyperactive at first. Will arch tail upward and forward as far as possible. Will back in almost perpendicular position against sides of tank, then relax and act normal. Then usually die in 15-20 minutes.	High salinity. More than 40 parts per thousand	Correct formulation of salt water.
In winter, lobster sluggish when placed in water. Dies within 24 hours. When boiled, meat—usually tail section—mushy.	Freezing. Ice crystals formed in tissue cells	Adequate protection in transit.
July to October, in new shell stock; lobster weakens and dies.	Weak stock. Lobsters more sensitive generally because of moulting and adverse holding conditions, especially too abrupt changes in temperature. May be further weakened by poor handling.	Handle lobsters as carefully as if they were eggs. Avoid any abrupt changes in physical and chemical environment.

The DO's and DO NOT's of Profitably Operating a Recirculated-Refrigerated Lobster Storage System

1. Do obtain lobsters from dealers who cull and condition lobsters during preshipment storage, and protect them adequately during storage.

2. Do select safe construction material for components of system. Safe metals—zinc, stainless steel and aluminum.

2. Do not use copper or copper alloys or lead-base paints.

3. Do select a pump of adequate size and of safe material.

3. Do not use pump with bronze impeller.

4. Do consult refrigeration engineer for size of refrigeration unit.

4. Do not use high speed jet pumps, or reduce pipe size on positive side of pump [gas poisoning].

5. Do give preference to new equipment over second-hand, especially refrigeration unit.

6. Do protect lobsters from direct contact with cooling surfaces.

7. Do maintain the filter.

8. Do plan your particular needs so you can determine accurately the size of system required.

8. Do not overcrowd lobsters. Two gallons water to one pound lobster considered best ratio.

9. Do change water when there is excessive foaming, water becomes foul smelling, or unsightly. Four teaspoons olive oil added drop by drop will temporarily correct foaming.

10. Do be careful about sanitation.

10. Do not feed lobsters.

11. Do remove lobster fragments, etc. from system as soon as possible.

11. Do not use aerosol insecticides in vicinity of tanks. (What will kill a fly, will kill a lobster much more quickly.)

12. Do check salt content of water periodically.

13. Do temper the lobsters to approximate the temperature of the system water.

Availability of Equipment. There are a number of firms which supply the whole equipment for artificial sea-water storage. One firm in Haverhill is expanding its sales into the middle west. It provides:

1. The tanks equipped with non-metallic piping
2. The refrigerator whose cooling coils are iron rather than copper
3. A filter system consisting of a wooden trough in which are laid batts of fibre glass, the same as used in insulating a house
4. The various salts composing its secret formula for sea water.

A user of this installation reports that its losses of lobsters are, if anything, slightly less than with natural sea water. They change the filters once a week (their water is pronouncedly murky) and the water once every three months. They use ordinary tap water for the mix.

The cost of an installation of a capacity of 9,000 gallons is in the neighborhood of $10,000. The charge for a new mixture of salts is approximately $120 (every three months).

V

Pounds

A pound, as referred to here, means a cove, dammed off from the sea, into which the tide ebbs and flows.

Lobster pounds came into general use after canning of lobsters was forbidden in Maine. A surplus of lobsters which formerly could be handled by canning had to be preserved by other means, and pounds were the answer.

This seasonal increase in the catch of lobsters is striking. Most Canadian lobsters are imported during the months of May and June, while the Maine landings are principally in August and September. Together, Canadian imports and Maine landings result in a peak supply during the period from May to September. An additional need for pounds is caused by the summer shedding season when soft-shelled lobsters are unattractive as food, and have high mortality in shipping.

Today, tidal pounds represent over two-thirds of the Maine live-lobster storage facilities, and are the best means for holding lobsters for several months without high mortalities.

The New England coast south of Cape Elizabeth (Portland) lacks a highly indented coast line and protective islands. This fact and the relatively small catch of lobsters means that the southerly coast is not suited to construction and use of tidal pounds. Practically all such pounds are located between eastern Casco Bay and Jonesport, with concentrations being generally located in the Boothbay, Bristol and Friendship areas.

> A pound will be filled with hard-shell lobsters when lobsters first become active in the spring and when Canadian imports are at their peak. Care must then be taken that the lobsters are taken out before the summer moulting time, for many captive lobsters that shed their shells are eaten by their companions. Pounding delays

the moult by several weeks by which time they command a premium over the newly-shed lobsters that are being caught. After the hard-shelled lobsters have been removed, the softer, newly-moulted lobsters from the landings are released in the pound. These lobsters harden as the summer progresses, and withstand the rigors of shipment better. During the summer, a pound may be almost continuously stocked and emptied, depending upon sales, landings, and condition of the lobsters.

In anticipation of the high prices prevailing in midwinter when landings fall to a very low point, lobster pounds are stocked to capacity in late summer or early fall when the combination of peak landings and dwindling markets result in the lowest prices of the year. Occasionally, a lapse in production results in a short period of high prices in late fall, at which time some pounds may be emptied to be refilled when the price drops again. Generally such a sharp fluctuation is caused by a stormy period which prevents fishing.[1]

It is obvious that a pound owner who can buy lobsters at a low price and hold them until the price is high will make a good deal of money.

But there are handicaps to an easy profit. In the first place, pounds are expensive to build. They cost $2,500 and up. Then the capital tied up in stocking a pound is considerable (perhaps 30,000 pounds at 70 cents per pound).

And *will* the market rise to a price higher than the cost?

But the greatest gamble depends on the mortality of the captive lobsters.

A loss of only 3 per cent is claimed by some pound owners, but this is unusual, and 10 to 15 per cent loss is about normal. Unfortunately, losses can run above 30 per cent, and sometimes the entire contents of the pound are lost. These heavy losses seem to run in epidemics.

---

[1] From Robert L. Dow, Donald M. Harriman, and Leslie W. Scattergood, "The Role of Holding Pounds in the Maine Lobster Industry" (Fish and Wildlife Service Bulletin No. 5), which has been used in preparation of this section.

The common causes of high pound losses are:

1. Overcrowding of the pound
2. Feeding putrid bait
3. Red Tail disease[2]
4. Shell disease
5. Weak lobsters
6. Wrong salinity and temperature of water

The first two causes can be readily overcome, but Red Tail is more serious, and there are other causes which lobster biologists have not been able to diagnose. Severe winter mortalities can occur when neither Red Tail nor Shell Disease can be detected.

On the whole, it might seem as though sloppy poundkeeping is responsible for high losses. Such is not the case. The most scrupulously tended pound may be infected with Red Tail; and of two adjoining pounds under the same ownership one may be cursed with a 30 per cent loss and the other with a 5 per cent loss.

Careful poundkeepers keep their pounds clean, and when they are empty of lobsters rake up all residue of bait, and even remove dead seaweed. But that is not enough. Today (1960), Sea and Shore Fisheries furnish men to direct the chlorination of a pound. This treatment disinfects the surface scum of the floor of the pound. It is this scum which carries most of the bacteria of Red Tail and other diseases. The chlorine is in the form of pellets which are scattered about two feet apart over the mud of the empty pound. The pound owner pays the cost of the pellets and furnishes the men to spread them. A pound of 35,000 to 40,000 pounds capacity of lobster will require four drums of chlorine at $40.00 per drum. Some poundkeepers chlorinate twice during the season, especially in times of threatened epidemic of Red Tail.

Flushing out the objectionable scum with a high pressure hose as a means of reducing bacteria is not recommended, at least not until *after* chlorination. The contam-

---

[2] *See* page 29.

inated scum would merely be washed into the harbor and could possibly spread the disease.

The bacteria of Red Tail is also present in bait barrels. This suggests that bait barrels should be chlorinated and well flushed out after each use.

Overcrowding. The capacity of a pound may not be the same from one year to the next. You cannot say that because you successfully stocked 40,000 pounds of lobster last year you can do it again this year. Variations in water temperature and in cleanliness of the pound determine its capacity. Most operators would have less mortality if they would use the available information on capacity as governed by sanitation.

Weak lobsters. An important factor is the vigorousness of the lobsters to be pounded. A pound located where lobsters can be bought directly from the fishermen usually fares better than if the lobsters have to be brought in by truck. In trucking, the lobsters are always crowded in crates and usually exposed to high temperatures.[3]

Salinity and temperature of water. Fish and Wildlife Service states:

> Except as it affects the lobsters' tolerance to high water temperatures and dissolved oxygen depletion, salinity does not seem to be a major problem in most pounds. The volume of fresh water required to reduce the salinity of the lobster pound to the danger point is more than is usually available. Occasionally, however, enough fresh water will flow over the top of a pound, sweeping away the higher layers of sea water, so that there is insufficient oxygen in the residual layer of sea water to support the lobsters. In this case, mortality is directly due to smothering. Specific gravity affords a ready means for making an approximate estimate of salinity (as the hydrometer used by auto service stations to test the specific gravity of storage battery solutions).

---

[3] *See* Acclimatization, page 102.

Since, however, density varies also with temperature, account has to be taken of this factor in making calculations.

Water temperatures appear to be a limiting factor in the Casco Bay area in Maine, and establish the western limit of lobster pounding. Here water temperatures rise to 65°F. or higher, and the commercial storage of lobsters becomes difficult.

Feeding

Pounded lobsters are usually fed, although they may go for several months in winter without feeding. Unfed, they lose weight, and cannibalism becomes more troublesome. Redfish racks [the scrap left after the fish are filleted] and herring are the most popular foods. Trash fish [not suitable for eating] may also be used. The amount of food given can be quite critical. If more is provided than the lobsters can eat, the resulting putrefaction consumes oxygen and may release toxic products. Food requirements vary with season and condition of lobsters; therefore, most poundkeepers provide just enough food so that none is left after twenty-four hours.[4]

A general rule is one bushel of feed per week per one thousand pounds of lobsters.

Location of pound. The location of a pound should preferably be a natural habitat of lobsters. A rocky shore is preferred, since the problem of silt is then reduced. A pound shaped like a finger extending inland from the sea is not desirable. Dr. Thomas states, " In such a pound, there is a tendency for the water which remains at low tide to be pushed to the landward end of the pound on flood tide, returning with the ebb, so that replenishment of the storage water is incomplete. This problem is particularly acute at the end farthest from the open sea."[5]

[4] Dow, Harriman, and Scattergood, *op. cit.*

[5] H. J. Thomas, " Lobster Storage."

British practices. Some pounds in Britain recognize the desire of lobsters to avoid light by providing shade through awnings in the water. The awnings are wooden platforms mounted about nine feet from the bottom of the pound, and the area so shaded is about one-third the total pound area. It must be difficult to recover the pounded lobsters if the awnings are fixed—the British often recover their lobsters by trapping them with baited scoops or pots, or by operators dressed in rubber suits working a push net. But if the awnings were floating rafts, they could be moved about to permit dragging. British pounds sometimes provide " hides " for lobsters on the bottom. These consist of stone slabs resting on bricks 4 to 6 inches off the bottom, and resembling a small bench seat.

In several Scottish pounds, a hospital tank is provided for weak lobsters. Fresh sea water is pumped into it at a rate to provide a complete change of tank water every hour. This tank is 19 feet by 1½ feet by 1 foot depth of water. Air is provided by a compressor, and is diffused into the water below a false bottom.

In " Lobster Storage " (published by The Scottish Home Department), it is noted that " the initial few days of storing are the most dangerous since the lobsters are adjusting, and are restless and more liable to fight over food and attack lobsters which are added. The latter are often somewhat weakened by travelling. If the claws are not secured, lobsters should be first accommodated in a section hived off from the main body. After a few days, during which the lobsters will settle, the separating partition can be removed."

VI

Shipping of Lobsters

The common container for shipping lobsters is a wooden barrel having a wooden box, or small keg, inside the barrel to hold the lobsters. Wet seaweed is packed with the lobsters, and the spaces around the inner wooden box are filled with crushed ice. The inner box should be reasonably watertight so that the melting ice cannot drip fresh water onto the lobsters, killing them. Occasionally a customer specifies that the cover of the inside keg be waterproof to prevent such leakage.

Rail Express. The express shipping of live lobsters is said to have originated by the desire of William Randolph Hearst to serve lobsters at his mansion in Colorado.

It is done successfully if the lobsters are carefully selected to be vigorous, and if provision is made by the express company to re-ice the container during transit. Care must be taken to place the ice either below the bed of lobsters or in the ice compartments surrounding them. Melting ice on top of them would drip fresh water onto the lobsters, killing them.

Today, several firms specialize in shipping live lobsters by Railway Express as far as the West Coast. Their guarantee that they will arrive alive or your money back covers an 1,800-mile distance.

Saltwater Farm of Maine has kindly furnished the following information:

> We are pioneers in the business of guaranteeing lobsters to arrive alive or your money back, and report that our losses average 1 per cent or slightly less. There are variations from year to year depending upon rail strikes, and severe weather.
>
> Live lobsters travel in Railway Express service under the live animal rate, which is, briefly stated, 150 per cent of first class rate billed in a 20-pound mini-

mum. Originally, Railway Express re-iced every 24 hours in transit, as needed, as a service within the premium rate. Re-icing charges were granted by the I. C. C. in 1956 and are assessed on the basis of net weight times distance traveled. Re-icing is charged by Railway Express Agency whether it is performed or not. On a winter's day, with insulated truck service to Boston and refrigerator service to Chicago, it is unlikely that re-icing is performed.

Railway Express Agency by no means guarantees replacement. Every claim is an individual fight, and every possible bit of small print in the I. C. C. Tariff Regulations is used to avoid payment of claims.

The number of false claims is negligible. In the first place, we refund promptly and in the event of a false claim this is embarrassing to the claimant. Railway Express, in its zeal to avoid payment of claims, investigates extremely thoroughly, and our own records are kept so that we can detect someone who requests replacement or refund more than once.

We ship very little to New England where lobsters are readily available, although we have a number of faithful customers even on Cape Cod and Nantucket who prefer our lobsters and our method of packing them.

We use the same sizes of container for the lobsters and clams, but use several different sizes of barrel. Distant shipments use large barrels with considerably more ice.

Our business is not seasonal. We ship every day of the year except Sundays. Because our containers are eminently adaptable to outdoor cooking and eating, there is an increase of business during the summer. The differential is none the less narrowing as the market spreads through the south and west. As an example, we can cite the month of March 1960, which, despite the bad weather in the vertical middle of the country, showed volume comparable to October and November.

This should also be true of April. We of course have brief peaks of volume at Christmas and particularly at New Year's Eve.

We handle shedding season by buying lobsters with a good shell on them to the extent possible, in the early part of the season from the areas where shedding has not yet reached, and in the latter part of the season from areas where shedding took place early. Lobsters with inadequate shell are culled out and pounded for shipment when their shell has been restored.

We feed our pounded lobsters herring and redfish racks [scrap]. When the water temperature lowers the lobster's appetite to zero, we cease feeding.

With our method of packing for cooking, wherein the customer need never touch the lobsters until they are ready to serve, we need to plug but one claw for protection of lobsters from their buddies.

Dry ice is much too cold to use as a refrigerant for lobsters. It freezes and kills them. Its staying power is relatively short and not suitable for shipments of any distance. When it evaporates, it releases about thirty times its volume in the form of carbon dioxide gas which kills the lobsters if the freezing does not. (Note: the intense cold cracks polyethylene wrappers, if used.)

We do ship by air. We do so when rail service is inadequate. Some of the places to which we have shipped where this is the case are Antwerp, Paris, Zurich, Caracas, Havana, Bermuda, Honolulu and Alaska. The percentage is small, as can be adduced by populations and income levels at such points.

We have never had a lobster shed during shipment, although we have had a few females that egged out. Shedding is an athletic business that takes place at fairly high temperatures in an unrestricted area. The lobster hasn't room to shed in a container; the cold inhibits it.

We don't know whether smaller lobsters stand travelling better than larger ones. We suspect that this is so, but we suspect it inferentially in that youth is better able to stand the stress than age.

This business was started in 1949 with a capital of $730.00, and today (1959) the sales of its products amount to about $500,000.

Trucking. Truck shipment of lobsters is not new. Only a few comments are of value.

The use of refrigerated trucks can be dangerous if the temperature of the truck body should become low enough to freeze and, of course, kill the cargo. Specify that it does not fall below 40°F. A cargo of lobsters packed in ice in an ordinary truck arrives in better shape than a refrigerated truck without ice. The melting ice provides moisture in the air which aids in keeping the lungs of the lobsters moist.

The shipping of lobsters in open crates in a refrigerated truck is dangerous. The air flowing from the refrigerating unit through the openings between the slats of the crates dries out the lobsters and causes high mortality. It is essential to use barrels or boxes which are not open-sided.

Shipments of a full load of lobsters (a small truck if necessary), and on a nonstop run, arrive much better than when the truck must stop frequently to pick up other cargo. Runs under such conditions as far away as Memphis, Tennessee, arrive with no loss in the cargo.

Air express. Most of this section has been contributed by Brooks-Sprague Corporation, of Massachusetts, who are credited with being the pioneer in air shipment of lobsters (about 1940):

> Our first container was a galvanized can with cover, but these were not satisfactory, so we switched to a corrugated box with a rubber liner which was returnable. Some newcomers in the field tried to ship with a cheaper package that was not leakproof. One of these shipments leaked so badly that the liquid ran through the plane and when it reached the cold air froze controls and wiring on the plane. We don't know just what the damages amounted to, but it was a very

expensive proposition, and the airlines clamped embargoes on all lobster shipments. [American Airlines reported $20,000 damage.] Capital Airlines will still not carry lobsters.

We finally came up with a package that was acceptable with the airlines, but was far from ideal from the shipper's standpoint. The airlines would not accept responsibility if they were less than seventy-two hours late in delivery, and this carton could not keep lobsters alive for that length of time.

As far as we know, the only requirements of the airlines is a nonleaking package. Some dealers are cutting corners in trying to reduce the cost of the package and we are afraid we will be faced with another embargo very soon when one of these cartons falls apart and leaks all over the plane.

We ship all over the country and the furthest points would be Vancouver, B. C.; Portland, Oregon; Los Angeles and San Francisco, California; Houston, Dallas, Corpus Christi and Galveston, Texas. Our percentage of loss since we reopened has been less than 1 per cent, but this is due to the care we take rather than the perfection of the carton.

We use ice with a chemical additive which is sealed in a polyethylene bag and leakproof.

As stated previously, the airlines will not accept responsibility under seventy-two hours, which is why we must have a better package. On rare occasions, weather conditions may force the plane to take on additional fuel somewhere along the way and the lobsters may be unloaded to make room for this additional weight. We have been fortunate in this respect, but with this possibility facing us we must find some way to protect each and every shipment.

The present container is almost airtight and the lobsters *do* suffer from lack of oxygen, which is a problem we are hoping to overcome with our new package. Lobsters are mostly carried in the baggage compartment or belly of the plane and as these are pressurized the altitude does not affect the lobsters too much. We do, however, have a new problem with the jet flights. On a recent jet flight shipment, the pilot took the plane to 30,000 feet to avoid poor weather; the temperature in the belly was down to minus thirty degrees, and the lobsters arrived badly.

Strange though it may seem, there are actually some cities in the country where we can ship by air cheaper than by rail. This is due mostly to the sharp drop in rates when you reach the hundred pound level. We would think, however, that air charges would average ten to fifteen per cent higher than railway charges.

We ship Canadian lobsters whenever they are available in preference to the Maine lobsters as they are stronger, harder shelled, and more fully meated. As a general rule, these lobsters will cost us more than the Maine lobster, but they are worth it. The lobsters are usually plugged by the fishermen as they catch them and we prefer to have both claws plugged so they will not damage each other.

No full place loads are required except when we have them flown to us from Newfoundland, at which time full or half loads of thirteen thousand or sixty-five hundred pounds is a minimum. The airlines will accept single packages, which usually are carried by passenger planes, although some are carried by air freighters.

Lobsters are shipped year-round but naturally we have better results in the winter and spring when the lobsters are in their best condition and cooler weather prevails. We concentrate mostly on smaller accounts which permit us a higher margin of profit.

There is only a cursory examination by the airlines to make sure the carton will not come apart in transit. We are very particular in the accounts we accept and accept the customer's word if he has any fault to find with the shipment. As we have yet to receive any false

> claims, we believe we are doing a fine job in selecting our clientele.
>
> Our insulated air packages hold fifty pounds of live lobsters, which must be considered a minimum order. Live lobsters are sized from one to five pounds each.

Consolidated Lobster Company also reports on air shipments:

> The airplane companies will assume responsibility for loss of lobsters if the plane is forced down from mechanical failure, but not if due to an unscheduled landing due to weather. As a result, we watch the weather reports before shipping. If the weather is bad either at Boston or on the route, we delay shipping.
>
> About 10 per cent of our shipments of lobsters are by air.
>
> We no longer use a canned refrigerant. It was too bulky and heavy. We now use the plastic bag containing ice and a chemical powder which lowers the temperature of the ice to 0°F.
>
> Our air shipments are mostly to Florida and west of the Mississippi River.

The loss in weight which always occurs in any method of shipping lobsters is due to the drainage of water from the gill chambers of the lobsters. This lost weight is recovered if they are stored in sea water after arrival.

The lobster industry owes much to American Airlines for its pioneering of air shipments. This company is usually credited with developing in conjunction with box manufacturers the modern corrugated-board waterproof container. American Airlines also promoted the sale of air-shipped lobsters to restaurants on the West Coast, offering them in a freshness never before possible.

Packing with Shavings. Several years ago, two Belgian seafood importers introduced the scheme of packing lobsters for shipment in *dry* wood shavings used under, over, and surrounding the lobsters. This was in place of the time-honored barrels with ice and seaweed. The saving in weight was phenomenal (50 pounds of lobsters packed the old way weighed 140 versus 58 pounds when packed with shavings). This packaging has not come into general use, probably because it does not preserve the lobsters well in summer, though it does suffice in the colder wintertime.

It is a real nuisance to remove the shavings.

Another experiment in shipping was to seal the live lobster in a transparent plastic bag into which some kind of gas had been introduced. The nature of the gas has not been learned, but it maintained the lobster alive though in suspended animation as if it were sleeping. When released from the bag the lobster (one test) appeared lively and was of good flavor. Apparently this process has been dropped.

VII

Preservation of Lobster Meat

Freezing. The freezing of live lobsters and shipping them frozen and whole has been tried in several Maine ports. It has not been successful.

It is claimed that the taste of frozen lobsters is not the same as live lobsters; that even boiled lobsters which have then been frozen for shipment are not as good as freshly boiled lobsters.

In at least one case, the lobsters were not deeply frozen quickly enough. *Quick* freezing is the backbone of the Birdseye process, and results in the cells of vegetables not being burst by the freezing but retaining their structure and flavor. Another difficulty in any frozen lobster is that it becomes very brittle so that it is almost impossible to maintain the claws attached to the body. One lobster firm broke the arms away and shipped the body in a tray with the claws lying alongside. It did not look like a lobster and had less appeal.

The Maine Agricultural Experiment Station found:

1. That meat sticks to the shell, and is difficult to remove in lobsters which have been frozen without any precooking

2. That lobsters which have been "heat treated" before freezing by steam cooking for seventy seconds at 195°F. can be readily shucked out of the shell, yet the color of the shell remains green or black. The cooking affects only the surface of the meat; the interior is still raw

3. That when lobsters are cooked at 212°F. for one minute or more before freezing, their color changes to orange or the familiar red of a cooked lobster. They have lost the green or black color of live lobsters.

The 195°F. cooking for seventy seconds was found to be the best treatment. The meat was easily removed from both claws and tail. The tail curled up tightly and was springy. It was frozen at -20°F. for forty-eight hours.

Similarly, complete lobsters were cooled at 60°F. after heat treatment and then frozen at -30°F. for twenty-four hours. Before storage they were given a glaze of a spray of water.

After three months' storage at -20°F., all samples except those completely cooked prior to freezing had good texture and flavor, and compared very favorably with freshly cooked lobster. The meat from claws that had been completely cooked prior to freezing was found to be fibrous and mealy in texture, and possessed a flavor inferior to that of fresh-cooked lobster meat. The tail section alone, either heat-treated or completely cooked and treated in 2 per cent salt brine, had a longer storage life than the whole lobster.[1]

Anti-biotics. In the March 17, 1956, issue of *The Saturday Evening Post* appeared an article " New Ways to Keep Food Fresh."

It tells of a refrigerated truckload with carcasses of thirty freshly killed steers to be trucked three hundred miles to Santiago, Cuba. While still two hundred miles away, the truck and its refrigerating unit broke down. It stayed by the side of the road all the first night, all the second day in the blazing sun, and the second night and most of the third day. Upon arrival it was, of course, expected that all of the meat would be putrid. And half of it was, but the fifteen carcasses of the other half were good, and surprisingly fresh. These fifteen steers had been injected with an anti-biotic (aureomycin) solution (only a few parts per million) immediately after slaughtering. (In later tests the injection came before slaughtering.) This chemical was developed largely through Dr. Hugh Tarr, at the Pacific Fisheries Experimental Station, in a search for a preservative for fish. Aureomycin was mixed in tiny amounts in the water to be frozen into ice and flaked for packing. A whole, ungutted fish was packed in this ice, and at the end of twelve days

[1] *See* " Processing Lobster and Lobster Meat for Freezing and Storage " (Bulletin No. 558).

was beautiful and edible. (Untreated fish at 40°F. was suspicious after three days, and reeked after five.)

Gutted chickens have been similarly treated with equally astonishing results. Notice that, while the steers were treated by pumping the anti-biotic through their blood vessels, both the fish and the chickens received their treatment from the outside and from the crushed ice. It is surprising how the chemical penetrated through the scales of the fish.

The benefits of anti-biotic treatment to lobster will be great when it can be accomplished.

Experiments in Canada were tried by immersing for a half-hour in an ice-cold anti-biotic solution whole lobsters as they came from the cooker. With a strong solution, lobsters were kept fresh to sixteen days while the untreated or control lobsters were spoiled on the eleventh day. Another gain is that such treated boiled lobsters could be shipped refrigerated by dry ice. Dry ice vapors (CO_2) will kill a living lobster. Compared with ice for refrigerant this would be a reduction in weight, and a reduction of damage from the spilling of the melted ice water (especially for airplane shipment).

The experiments on treated steers and chickens have been made on degutted animals, but it is not practical to degut a lobster. Experiments have been conducted at the plant of Consolidated Lobster Company to find a way to make the anti-biotic reach all through a lobster including its gut. The obvious approach is to inject the chemical into the blood stream of the living lobster, to be carried to all parts of its body. Injecting by a hypodermic needle is impractical, so the experiment was made by coating lobster plugs with aureomycin either as a powder stuck on with molasses (air dried) or with a very strong solution. The lobsters were killed by steam after allowing twenty minutes for the blood to circulate. Steam was used because it will kill the lobster without cooking it, and heating the anti-biotic will largely destroy its effectiveness. The lobster had to be killed since its normal bowel movement would eliminate the chemical after a few days.

Live lobsters were also immersed in tanks filled with a solution of anti-biotic in the hope that it would be absorbed through the lobster's shell, or its mouth. They were similarly killed by steam.

Untreated control lobsters were also killed, and both kinds stored on ice. There was no appreciable difference in keeping qualities between the two kinds. It appeared as though the anti-biotic had not penetrated.

Aureomycin has yet to be approved for lobsters by the Food and Drug Administration. It has been approved for chickens, and it now seems probable that it will be approved for all creatures which are to be cooked, as cooking removes even traces of the anti-biotic.

Freeze Drying. In *Time* of May 20, 1957, appeared an article on a new method of preserving food.[2]

> Dehydrated foods, never much admired, may be headed for kitchen fame. This week Dr. A. Copson of Raytheon Manufacturing Co. showed dried shrimp, lobster tails, strawberries, etc., that actually taste fresher than many fresh ones.
>
> A Raytheon dried shrimp is no shriveled, leathery remnant. It is nearly as big as a fresh peeled shrimp and made of a strange, brittle material with the consistency of popcorn or puffed cereal. Taken out of an airtight plastic envelope, it smells like raw shrimp, and its color is about the same. When one of these brittle ghosts is dropped into tepid water, it softens quickly and swells a little. After half an hour of soaking and two minutes in boiling water, the shrimp is firm, sweet and tastes like a shrimp that has been carefully preserved by freezing.
>
> Dr. Copson explained that it is all done by freeze-drying. When a material that contains water is frozen and placed in a vacuum chamber, the ice crystals in it sublime, i.e., turn directly into water vapor without melting to water. Pharmaceutical manufacturers use

[2] Reprinted through courtesy of *Time* (© Time, Inc., 1957)

freeze-drying to preserve sensitive drugs, but the process is difficult and it had never been successfully adapted to low-cost materials like foods. Another difficulty is that a considerable amount of heat (heat of sublimation) is required to evaporate the ice crystals. This heat must reach the center of the material, and in the case of most foods the evaporation of crystals near the surface forms a layer of corklike stuff that is an excellent insulator. It keeps heat of sublimation from reaching the interior unless the surface temperature is raised so high that the food spoils.

Raytheon gets around this problem by putting frozen foods in a vacuum chamber and shooting through them a powerful blast of ultra high-frequency radio energy. The waves agitate the molecules in the interior of the food and generate just enough heat to make the ice crystals turn directly into water vapor. If the job is handled properly, the food loses up to nine-tenths of its weight and turns into a brittle sort of substance while staying far below the freezing point. Chemical changes, which would damage flavor, cannot take place. Even unstable vitamins are preserved.

Raytheon regards its new process as experimental, and it does not know yet how long freeze-dried foods will keep at room temperature. They can be stored in plastic envelopes filled with nitrogen to prevent oxidation, but in the case of meat that contains fat there may be a tendency to deteriorate with time. Elaborate tests are now in progress to find the best ways to package and store them.

Cautious Raytheon men do not want to predict what effect freeze-drying will have commercially. But they point out that freeze-dried foods can be shipped without costly refrigeration and stored on grocers' or housewives' shelves.

One of the largest lobster companies has experimented with this or a similar process. It reports that the results were " somewhat less than satisfactory." A jury of tasters agreed that the lobster meat was rather tasteless and tough.

The High Voltage Engineering Company has developed a process of sterilizing lobster meat by the radiation of high voltage electricity. An early report (1960) on the results of this process states that the meat is less tough than with the Raytheon process but also that it is rather tasteless.

Most new processes were unsatisfactory at their beginnings; perhaps either of these methods may develop into an acceptable way of preserving lobsters.

VIII

Pacific Coast Transplanting

Fish and Wildlife Service states:

A number of attempts have been made to establish the American lobster to the Pacific coast. In the years 1874, 1879, 1888, and 1899, some 104,000 larvae and 355 adult lobsters were planted in California waters, and 233 adults were released in Puget Sound and off the mouth of the Columbia River in Washington. Also, two lobsters were released in Great Salt Lake, Utah. All of these transfers were unsuccessful. Between 1906 and 1917, efforts to transplant lobsters were intensified. A total of 24,572 lobsters were planted in Puget Sound, Washington, and 1,532 in Yaquina Bay, Oregon. It is evident that these lobsters also failed to survive and reproduce. In 1954, however, introductions of American lobsters to waters near Prince Rupert, British Columbia, met with some success. Several lobsters have been caught two years after being released. One individual was taken twenty miles from where it was planted. Thus, it has now been shown that the lobsters can be transplanted to Pacific water.[1]

One problem in estimating results has been the scarcity of persons who know what the Eastern lobster looks like. It has been easy to receive reports of catching lobsters, only to find that the catch was actually crawfish.

The ultimate success of this transplantation is yet to be determined.

Artificial Rearing of Lobsters[2]

Lobster hatcheries are not new; all the New England States except Vermont and New Hampshire have tried their

---

[1] "The American Lobster" (Bulletin No. 74), Fish and Wildlife Service.

[2] Ernest W. Barnes, Bulletin, House No. 2051, Massachusetts Division of Fisheries and Game, was used in preparation of this section. Much help also came from John Hughes, Director of the Oak Bluffs Hatchery.

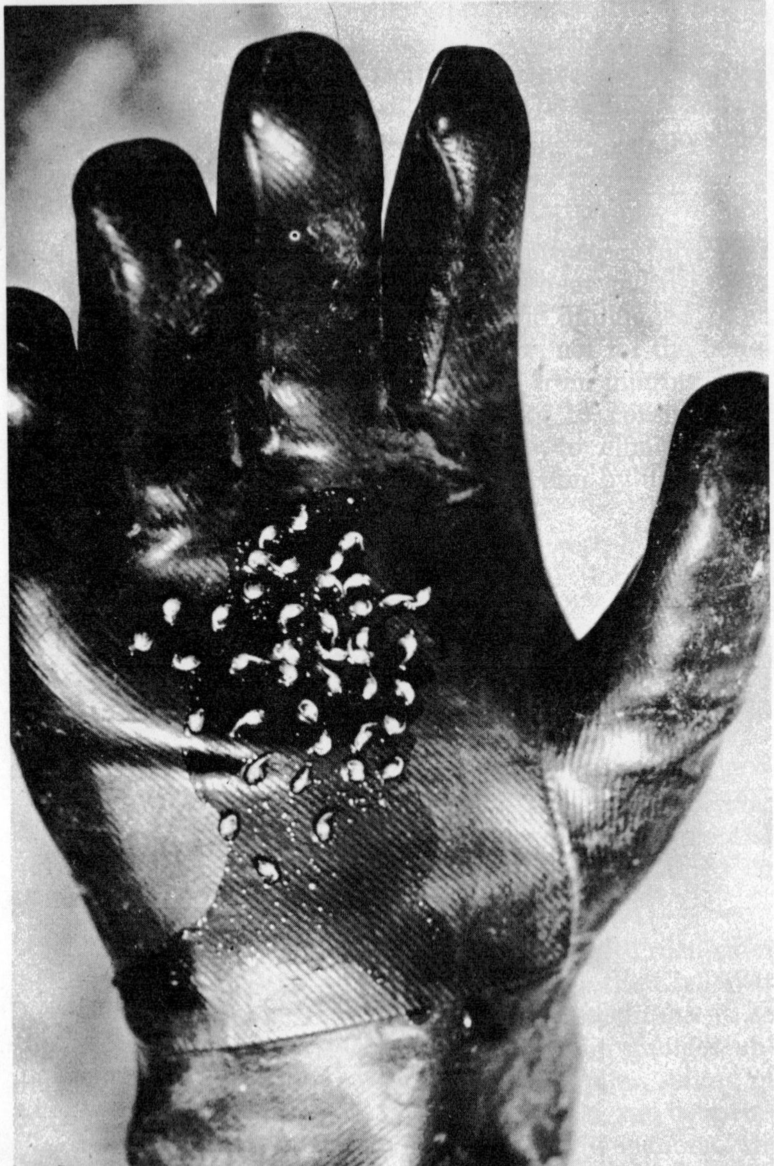

Fig. 17. One-day-old lobsters, ready for first shedding

hands at it. Rhode Island was perhaps the earliest. Today (1960) only Massachusetts, at its Oak Bluffs (Martha's Vineyard) station, hatches and raises lobsters through the fourth stage.

To understand the benefits of and problems of rearing lobsters, it is necessary to know the facts about them.

The female lobster extrudes her eggs onto the underside of the jointed part of her body and sticks them to the swimmerets located there. There will be perhaps five thousand eggs and up, and they resemble caviar. She carries the eggs nine or ten months, and must be constantly on guard against marauding fish which seek to steal the exposed eggs and at the same time must control her own movements lest the eggs be scraped off on the rocks. A high per cent of the eggs eventually hatch into tiny mosquito-like larvae.

Upon hatching from the egg, the young lobster swims helplessly near the top of the water for a period of from ten to thirty days, depending upon the temperature of the water. The swimming resembles "treading water" rather than actual vigorous, directional, swimming. During this period of heavy, aimless swimming it does not have the characteristic form of the adult lobster, but resembles more nearly a tiny shrimp, and, in addition to its tiny size, is in further jeopardy due to the fact that while in this helpless state it sheds its shell three times (see Figure 17).

In Massachusetts waters, these juveniles may go through eight to eleven molts in their first year of life, the annual number becoming progressively smaller with increasing age.

Each stage—representing the time between molts—has a characteristic form. In the first three stages the young lobsters are especially delicate and exhibit extreme cannibalistic tendencies, appearing to prefer to feed on each other than on any other kind of food. They do not have the usual instincts of caution or protection which are so pronounced in the adult lobster, but swim headlong into obstacles and dangerous looking situations. In passing into the fourth stage, the young lobster takes on a shape quite similar to that of the adult. In the early part of this stage, it swims vigorously with very evident direction, cautiously avoiding danger; and in the latter part of this stage it commences its life on the bottom, gradually giving up its swimming habits. The tiny lobsters which survive the first four stages and reach the bottom have a very much greater chance of surviving, since they instinctively hide under shells or between rocks.

As might be expected, because of the hazardous conditions in which they live, even under the best conditions in nature, not many reach this fourth stage. In extreme mortality, therefore, this represents the most critical period of their existence.

The problem of propagation is, therefore, to rear them through the first four stages, protect them from natural enemies, and, by feeding them heavily and by keeping them separate from each other by the use of proper currents of water, prevent or discourage cannibalism.

Once they take up their life on the bottom, the queer little larvae all at once begin to look and act like lobsters. The large claws which have been gradually making their appearance, become prominent, and the baby lobster immediately searches for places to hide on the ocean floor. It now has a chance to escape from its enemies.

This history shows why the rearing of lobsters ★★ through the fourth stage (¾″ to 1″ long) is so important. It is estimated that in nature only one-tenth of one per cent of hatched eggs reach the fourth stage yet in the Oaks Bluff hatchery approximately 30 per cent survive.

It was originally required by law that Massachusetts hatchery fry must be released in approximately the same waters where the mother lobster was caught. This was to prevent depletion of any area from which seed lobsters were taken, and also because through ages of evolution, the mother lobster, throughout the time of carrying her eggs and especially when the period of their hatching begins, frequents those areas within her range of travel that will provide the greatest protection for both eggs and young.

Today the seed lobsters at Oak Bluffs come from trawling and from depths and distances where it is not possible to replace the fry. As a result, these hatchery fourth-stage lobsters can be placed anywhere, and it is possible to restock any desired location.

Oak Bluffs was chosen for a hatchery because of its warmer waters and proper salt content. Warmer water assists in the speedier growth of small lobsters, permitting them to molt more often and reach the fourth stage sooner.

Hatching lobsters is a highly seasonal business, lasting only through one-half the year, for female lobsters hatch their eggs only through the warmer months. To be a year-round institution, the Oak Bluffs plant must primarily be a research plant devoted to shellfish investigations as well as to lobsters. Their work has evolved methods of circulating the sea water in their tanks in such a way as to keep the fry moving to discourage cannibalism, yet not to injure them by forcing them against the outlet screens. Plenty of food is provided to distract their cannibal traits. In Oak Bluffs, the food is ground quahog instead of the usual ground liver. Ground clams do not decay as quickly as liver, and the fouling of the tanks is less likely.

The results of stocking coastal waters with fourth-stage lobsters are very difficult to prove exactly.

Ernest W. Barnes, of the Massachusetts Division of Fisheries and Game, states:

> It is especially difficult to do so in the case of lobsters, since it requires at least five years before they reach the legal size and the effects of planting become known. However, such data as we have on the catch of lobsters in Rhode Island, where lobster propagation has been carried on for many years, show very definitely that the decline in the catch of lobsters was halted within five to six years after lobsters had been released from the rearing plant in quantities in excess of 500,000. It is further significant that this increase was especially noticeable in those areas which, because of their nearness to the hatchery, received the largest supply of

young. That the catch in other and neighboring states did not show this increase lends added significance to the above fact.[3]

Maine's Sea and Shore Fisheries point out that the number of fry released does not necessarily result in an increase of young lobsters. Hatchery experiences show that the present hatching and rearing methods are not as efficient as could be desired. If better methods can be discovered the conditions can be improved.

Oak Bluffs production of fourth-stage lobsters is only 200,000 a year. In the past, Rhode Island has had an annual yield of 1,000,000 such lobster fry, yet compare the smallness of Rhode Island's coast with that of Massachusetts. It is a pity that its production is so small, and the Oak Bluffs Director, John Hughes, hopefully dreams of using some of the salt-water ponds on Martha's Vineyard for large-scale hatching. Here is a need for lobstermen to band together to obtain a more suitable appropriation for the work.

The mortality of seed bearing lobsters in bringing them to a hatchery is great, perhaps 30 per cent; but it is more than offset by the benefits of a rearing plant. There is no way to prevent seed lobsters from entering a pot, but today's tendency is for lobstermen to release them in the locality where they are caught rather than bring them ashore for purchase and marking by state inspectors, then to be released in waters which may be highly unsuited to hatching.

" The artificial rearing of lobsters to the bottom-seeking stages," says Mr. Barnes, " should be included in any plan looking toward the re-invigoration of the lobster industry."[4]

The hatchery in Rhode Island went out of business due to a hurricane. In Federal Government hatcheries and those of other states, it was necessary to heat the water, and it became too expensive to continue.

" The time is already at hand," concludes Mr. Barnes, " when, in common with all other coastal marine fisheries,

---

[3] Barnes, *op. cit.*
[4] *Ibid.*

the lobster industry must be looked upon, not as a natural resource of unlimited proportions to be exploited as the immediate consideration dictates, but as a sea-farming activity which—no matter how extensive the grazing area may now seem, the abundance, nevertheless, has very definite limits —may easily be destroyed; and a sufficient supply of growing stock must be retained if we are to maintain the desired yield."[5]

[5] *Ibid.*

IX

Marketing

The marketing of lobsters has shown little change in one hundred years. The exceptions are the lobstermen's cooperatives, the specialty selling, such as Salt Water Farm, airplane shipments, artificial sea water, and the search for new means of preserving lobster meat. It is time to take a long hard look at some of the outgrown practices of the industry.

Marketing covers many phases of lobstering other than selling. Included are:

1. Moving lobsters to consumers in the desired form and conditions at the lowest possible cost
2. Making a living for lobstermen and dealers, through a reasonable return for the money and effort expended
3. Finding new markets, new lobster products, or more of the old products.

The lobsterman himself is directly involved in only the second function; for the others he has to depend on someone else. He often overlooks this dependence, and resents the added expense—" The lobster I sell for 70 cents ends up in a restaurant on a $4.00 dinner, or in a fish market for $1.50."

What determines the price? Supply and demand, of course. The daily (blue) lobster price bulletin put out in Boston by the Department of the Interior, Bureau of Commercial Fisheries, is a factor, as is the green sheet published in New York. It is based on inquiries among many lobster wholesalers as to what they are paying that day and is intended to be a representative cross-section of lobster prices in New England. The prices on the green sheet are for lobsters landed in New York and are about 10c per pound higher than F.O.B. Maine.

The morning telephone gossip among buyers is probably the biggest factor in arriving at a price. They learn that Joe

Doakes has refused an offer of 65 cents from New York, that another buyer has picked up 3,000 pounds from Jonesport at 67 cents, but rumor is that there are a lot of tired lobsters in the shipment, that a three-day storm off Cutler has kept lobstermen at home for several days, and that the catch off Boothbay is so poor that the lobstermen are only hauling every other day. All signs point to a price of 75 cents or better. On the other hand, Bill Smith has sold off his larger lobsters and is loaded up with chicken lobsters, and he hears that the per cent of small lobsters in the average catch is running unusually high. He'd better unload—even at a loss—and have his tanks and capital ready for a better buy. So chicken lobsters are offered retail by the chain stores at less than the lobstermen were paid.

This is an example of the unfavorable market trends where a glut of production frequently causes small dealers with limited capital and storage facilities to have to dump their lobsters at distress prices so that they may continue to meet their buying commitments.

Another factor which affects the prices of lobsters—especially lobster meat—is the variation in fishing laws between the United States and certain provinces of Canada. This refers to the low-priced lobster meat produced in New Brunswick, so low that United States lobster dealers cannot compete, nor can even other sections of Canada.

If the wholesale price is correct, then lobsters will move freely to consumers (even if the price is high). But if it is out of line, buying slows down and there is a glut. What the consumer will pay is usually first noted by the wholesaler, and works downward to the lobsterman. The wholesaler, to a large extent, regulates the market price. He is a key figure in the assembly and distribution of lobsters.

A good marketing system can help achieve fuller use of the lobsters that are caught. It can cut down lobster mortality and deterioration through new and better methods of storage, packing, and handling. It can find by-product uses for parts of the lobster which now are wasted. Storage and processing improvements can provide fuller use of a lobsterman's gear, and help to iron out the seasonal nature of the industry. The expense of transportation can be reduced, partly by reducing the bulk of lobster (and ice) shipments, and partly by spreading the shipping season over a greater part of the year. Two experimental methods of processing lobsters have been described.[1] They have not yet been successful, but they point the way toward better marketing.

Some lobstermen resent the profit of the man to whom they sell. "The buyer doesn't have to put out in vile weather. *He* doesn't have to stand the loss of gear in a storm. *He* doesn't have to carry the loss when the catch is so poor that it doesn't pay for the gas. Yet he makes a lot better living than I do." All this is true, and a simpler system of marketing would be desirable. But roadside stands and door-to-door peddling, which would work when the industry was small, won't work today. It is impractical for the lobsterman to deal with the consumer. Now, the lobsterman loses track of his catch. His lobsters are resold several times, and several middlemen are involved. The buyer has his griefs too, and must be paid for his contribution to the chain of marketing to ensure that the lobsters reach the consumer in the desired form. He has to absorb culls and dead lobsters (sometimes a high percentage), furnish the capital to pay the lobsterman on delivery, sell gear (often at cost), supply bait, grade the catch, furnish ice and transportation, and take the gamble that he can sell his lobsters at a profit. He is a necessary link in the chain.

The dealer takes the biggest gamble. Granted that the lobsterman risks loss of his traps in a storm, but the money in his catch has a quick turnover. He handles hundreds of pounds of lobster per week against the thousands of pounds of a dealer. He sells for cash, usually at a flat pound price without deduction for one-clawed or even weak lobsters.

The buyer naturally wants to buy as cheaply as possible and sell for as much as he can, and this understandable attitude irks many lobstermen, who often think their buyers

---

[1] *See* pages 123-28.

are whittling them down. But lobstermen in general seem to have very little real interest in the buyer's situation and his problems. If suddenly all buyers went out of business, the lobsterman would find himself up to his ears in lobsters, and no place to sell them. Remember that a buyer often has to purchase lobsters when he doesn't want to, and sell them at prices that are too low. If he doesn't do this, he could not prevent a glut of lobsters—and still lower prices. And the buyer would lose his clientele of lobstermen.

This is not to imply that the middlemen's profits are too high or too low. In making such a judgment, one should consider returns on invested capital in relation to the returns on invested capital in other comparable industries. If the returns are comparable, the needed capital will be attracted, and there will be more buyers to bid for the lobsters.

Startling evidence that the lobster industry is not advancing as it should is based on this statement on farm practices: More full-time workers were engaged in 1953 in marketing farm products than in producing them. During the last twenty years, the number of workers in agriculture has gone down about 30 per cent, while the number in marketing may have increased by as much as one-third.

Compare this with the lobster industry. Has the number of men required to catch 1,000 pounds of lobsters been appreciably reduced? It does not seem likely. Then, can one deduce that the science of lobster catching is standing still? A common complaint in the industry is that there are too many lobstermen, and nobody makes a good living. If improvements in fishing can be devised, then fewer men can catch as many lobsters as before, and make a better living.

Another angle in marketing is to find new markets. Take crabs, for instance. Can the market for crabmeat be increased? Some people prefer it to lobstermeat, and the same gear that catches lobster can catch crabs. Could a lobsterman increase the dollar value of his day's haul by fishing for crabs also? Already this marketing is being practiced by some lobstermen.

Standards. Other industries have recognized standards for their products, and the seller lives up to these standards, and guarantees they are a specified grade. The lobster industry has a few standards such as " large," " select," " chicken," and " culls." But there is no designation showing how many days since a lobster has molted, i.e., how soft is its shell, or how many days it has been kept in a tank or pound, i.e., how freshly caught, or any designation from how deep water it has come (anyone would prefer a lobster from the deep, cold water of Maine to one caught in the warmer, shallow water of Hingham Harbor), or even if lobster meat comes from a freshly cooked, vigorous specimen or from a tired lobster culled out of a tank. This lack of standards benefits the careless handler, or the unscrupulous dealer. So poor are the standards that South African lobster tails are commonly advertised and sold as lobster meat—and they are not lobsters at all, but crawfish.

When dealers can be brought together to agree on designations for different grades, the whole industry will benefit.

Premium lobsters. Some districts catch premium lobsters, usually so called because they are larger. There isn't much the lobsterman can do about this, unless the supposedly larger size of Monhegan lobsters is due to the voluntary limitations of the fishing season. In contrast, there are a few harbors which have the reputation of an inferior catch—too many culls. The middleman can aid in the production of premium lobsters. Of course, he can do this by buying the fresher, stronger catch, but he can also do it by greater care in handling and storing them in his tanks. It is surprising to see the large number of dead lobsters removed in the morning from one buyer's tanks as compared with those of a buyer who handles them better. This is a matter of education.

A careful buyer will take note of how the lobsterman handles his catch. A few topnotch lobstermen keep a half barrel in their cockpits and pump sea water into it continuously. The lobsters go into this barrel as soon as they are plugged. Compare this method and its effect on the lobsters with the common method of dropping them into a basket. True, they are usually protected from the sun by a canvas cover, but they are in the hot summer air for much of the day, and unquestionably weakened. Buying from the lobsterman who keeps his lobsters in water would help the reputation of the buyer, i.e., his lobsters would be premium and would arrive in better shape at their destination.

Education again, and that is part of marketing.

Waste and spoilage. The perishable food of all kinds lost between the farm and the kitchen would feed millions of people. Spoilage by bacteria and molds, damage from rough handling, and deterioration in the quality all take their toll.

The same applies to lobstering, and the fault extends all down the line, from the lobsterman who roughly chucks his shorts overboard to fall with a splash on the water, or does not take pains to gently put a seed lobster back into the sea; to the buyer who harshly pulls apart two lobsters that are clinging together, or overloads his tanks, or does not keep his pound clean; to the wholesaler who doesn't ice his shipments adequately, or doesn't tank his lobsters before shipping.[2] All these are to blame.

It is sad to watch how some lobster buyers pack their lobsters in crates for shipping. It is not known why a shipper feels he has to cram each crate so full that the lid has to be pressed down. Granted that some of the lobsters will be shaken down by the jarring of the truck en route to their destination, but some of them must travel in distorted and unnatural positions. This cannot be good for them. Undoubtedly some of them are in a pretty moribund condition by the time the crates are pried open. Undoubtedly some of these never reach the customer.

Much has been done to combat waste, such as the use of better shipping containers and refrigerated trucks, better control of disease, better methods of holding lobsters in tanks

---

[2] *See* page 36.

and pounds—but there is still a high mortality, and much of it is due to ignorance or carelessness.

Canada seems to be ahead of the United States in using more of the lobster; some dealers even pool their boiled trash and have it picked up on a regular schedule for conversion into fertilizer. It is reported that Canada has developed a vacuum tool to separate carapace meat from the cartilage, and put up lobster legs in packages for ready sale.

Some fruits, such as cantaloupes, need to be ripened after they reach their destination, and are put into ripening rooms of controlled temperature and humidity. It is an excellent marketing practice to make sure that the fruit reaches consumers in the condition they want it. Similarly, it might be good practice to tank lobsters after their trip to a city to revitalize them. Such a tank could have natural or artificial sea water mixed with a plentiful supply of air or even oxygen.

Branding. An important aspect of merchandising is the marking of a particularly good product with a brand name as an essential to enable the customer to recognize a superior product. A brand name is assisted by a distinctive package. Whole lobsters are not readily adapted to packaging, but processed lobster products are.

The State of Maine has been desirous of marking its product as "Maine Lobster," and several years ago furnished lobstermen free with rubber bands, each carrying a two-color plastic plate printed "State of Maine Lobster." (See Figure 18.)

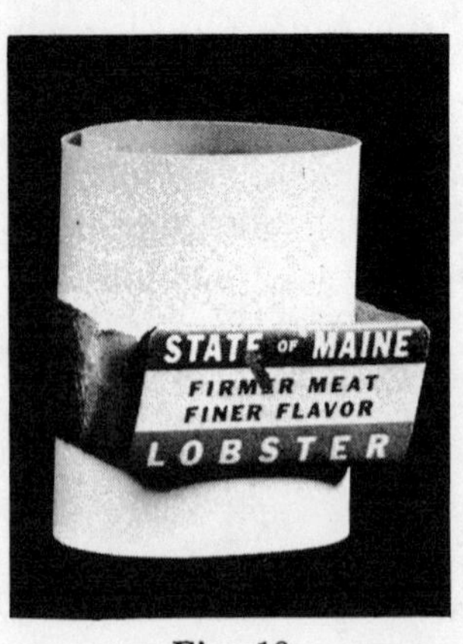

Fig. 18

This was a real step forward in better merchandising. These rubber bands were to be used in place of plugs in securing a lobster's big claw, and they were good, in that banding is better than plugging, which injures the claw; and especially because they identified the product. But they were impractical because lobstermen found them too hard to apply (there were then no tongs to expand them), and would not use them. Anyone who has seen a freshly caught lobster, fighting mad, rearing back with his claws wide open, can see how difficult it is to expand the elastic and slip it over the claw.

Fig. 19

Fig. 20

Another method of branding is shown in Figures 19 and 20. These are two samples of printed metal disks to be snapped over the tail of a lobster. Each has a locking tongue which pierces the tail and holds it in place. They were much easier to apply than the bands but were expensive. Notice that these are private name brands.

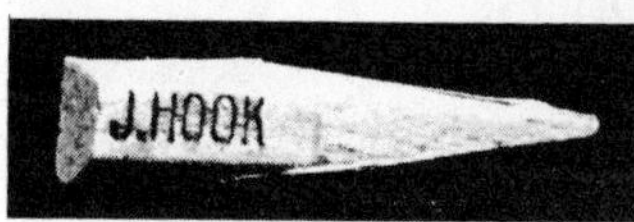

Fig. 21

Several years ago, wooden plugs were sold, each having the word "Maine" burned into them. They seemed to be a solution of branding since they required no extra labor. A lobster is going to be plugged anyway, so why not use a branded plug? They were not widely enough accepted to make their manufacture profitable (the plug shown in Figure 21 is a private brand).

A fourth branding method, tried only in a limited way, was the use of decalcomania, or transfers, whereby printing is transferred from a carrying sheet to any object desired. They were excellent; they were intended to be applied to the carapace or solid shell of the lobster. But their application was far too slow to be practical.

A fifth way of marking a lobster is the device used by

the state fisheries to tag them to test migration. This is a metal tag having one end bent over to form a hook to be caught under the back end of the carapace. The other end of the tag is fastened to an elastic band which in turn is slipped over the beak of the lobster. It is easy to apply, it will stay in place and does not injure the lobster.

"Sealedsweet" oysters have been marketed with a metal seal on each oyster, threaded through holes in the lips of both shells. It was expensive, but it labeled the product.

That none of these devices is in use today does not change the fact that they were the finest sort of marketing practice.

They were not adopted because they were difficult to apply or too expensive. Yet some branding device is necessary if advertising lobsters is ever seriously undertaken. Again, the problem seems to simmer down to education among the lobstermen and the buyers. If they could be shown how much branding would help them, then they might cooperate.

A brand name is one of the few ways that the United States lobster industry could combat the influx of Canadian lobsters with their competitive low prices.

Brand names are in use on a few lobster products, such as the "Ocean Clear" trade name of Consolidated Lobster Company, or the name "Saltwater Farm." Both firms are good merchandisers.

Advertising. Once an industry has a fine product and a brand name, it is in condition to advertise. The old saying that if you build a better mousetrap, though you live in the middle of the woods, you will have a beaten path to your door, just is not so. Unless the buyer learns of your product, and how superior it is, you are going to have a small business.

The lobster industry is going to have the importance of advertising forced down its throat. In fact, it already has; witness the attractive colored advertisements of South African Lobster Tails.

Advertising is expensive but has proven over and over again to yield big profits beyond its cost. It is doubtful if any state would pay for the advertising expense for any one industry, but if the lobstermen and buyers could be brought together *and educated,* they could raise the funds by a voluntary small tax on each lobster. Approximately 25 million lobsters (1960) are caught in Maine per year. One-half of one cent tax on each lobster would raise an advertising fund of $125,000. Does anyone raise their eyebrow in amusement at such an impractical idea? Yet something similar *has* been done, and among the same sort of folk as the lobstermen. The Maine potato growers banded together, voluntarily put a tax on each bag of potatoes, and hired a top-notch advertising firm to handle their campaign – with heartening results.

It can be done.

An example of what advertising might do is to educate doctors and the public that lobsters afford perhaps the best and certainly the most palatable way of introducing phosphorus into the human body.[3] Calcium phosphate forms about 58 per cent of bones, which owe their rigidity to its presence. In young animals phosphorus has a remarkable influence on the growth of bones. Owing to this influence, it has been used in the treatment of rickets. Its most effective use, however, is as a nerve tonic in paralysis agitans, locomotor ataxia, impotence, and nervous exhaustion. Yet very few people know this.

Another help from advertising would be to establish in the public mind that two chicken lobsters are preferable to one larger lobster. Some restaurants serve two chicken lobsters this way, but the buyer has not been sold on the fact that they are as desirable.

The Annual Lobster Festival in Rockland, Maine, is an advertising venture; but it doesn't reach many people, and it doesn't take advantage of the opportunity to educate those it does reach, on the handling of lobsters or how to open them or in what forms lobster can be bought.

---

[3] *See* page 28.

The displaying of living lobsters in a tank is excellent advertising, but it has not been exploited sufficiently. A display tank should be visible from the sidewalk, without requiring an observer to enter the store. The modern knowledge of how to use artificial sea water makes this possible.

Consumer wants. Not much thought has been given to how consumers would like lobster to reach them.

It is probable that women are the principal buyers of lobsters, yet many women are afraid of them and dread to handle them because of the threat of one unplugged claw. Lobsters are now plugged in the big claw, not for the benefit of the consumer, but to prevent them from injuring each other. It would be good merchandising to consider the housewife, and secure *both claws;* also to eliminate the black meat in claws caused by plug infection by using rubber bands instead of plugs.[4]

Is there a better way of delivering a fresh lobster than alive? Few kitchens are equipped with lobster shears which make it easy to open the shell, and there must be many a woman who is unskilled in handling a knife to slit open the body and break the claws. Poultry is sold freshly cooked and all cut up, needing only rewarming. Does this suggest any better way of selling a lobster?

Numerous printed instructions on how to open a lobster have been published, but how often do such instructions reach the buyer? This may mean that there are potential buyers who do not purchase because they are stumped on how to open a lobster.

Cooperatives. Lobster cooperatives are patterned after farmers' granges, which were established after the Civil War as a fraternal organization to improve farm conditions. The amazing number of 24,000 were formed. The granges undertook the purchase of implements and supplies, selling of farm products and operation of grain elevators, ran cooperative stores; and even went into banking and the manufacture of farm machinery. Many of them were not truly coopera-

---

[4] *See* page 56ff.

tive in that their earnings were distributed on the basis of stock holding rather than patronage. This factor contributed to the short life of many of them.

The old belief that a farmer's business interests should end at his front gate still was strong in 1900, and this belief is still shared by many lobstermen. On the other hand, farmers learned much about business methods in their early attempts to cooperate. They also tasted the strength of organization and acquired cooperative experience that their fathers did not possess.

The loss in 1960, during the hurricane, of all the tanked lobsters held by the Massachusetts cooperative in Scituate must have been an eloquent, though painful, lesson of the risks which dealers take.

Some lobstermen's cooperatives were formed primarily as purchasing agencies; they could buy a whole truckload of bait at a wholesale price, without having to give up several days' fishing each month to go after bait. Moreover, they were much more certain of getting their bait than any individual lobsterman could be. In addition, they could purchase warp and other gear at better prices. Today, most cooperatives buy the lobsterman's catch, paying cash as do other lobster buyers, and handling the sale of the lobsters.

There are five lobster cooperatives in Maine, and one large one in Massachusetts. They are a definite step forward towards uniting many men's interests, thereby multiplying their strength. They have the opportunity to band together and exert better marketing practices, something the other lobster buyers have not been able to do. Their success depends on their ability to obtain able managers, and on such control that lobstermen are obliged to trust one another. When lobster buyers tried in the past to join forces, they found that members could not be trusted to live up to their mutual agreements, and the union fell apart. This lack of trust is one of the biggest weaknesses among lobstermen. If anyone is a more rugged individualist than a lobsterman, he'd be hard to find. If anyone suggests that he give up an iota of his freedom, he will bristle with indignation and tell you where to go. On the other hand, he will go out of his way to help a fellow in distress; he might even rescue a drowning dealer, just so he can keep griping about him. The hope for branded lobsters, better standards of grading, and taxes for advertising rests on educating these organizations of lobstermen into seeing the benefits to be gained.

There are usually some valuable by-products of successful cooperative performance other than the dollars and cents values. Lobstermen, through their active part in owning and operating their own marketing machinery, have a better understanding of the away-from-home aspects of commerce.

The North Atlantic Lobster Institute was a cooperative of lobster dealers from Canada, Maine, and Massachusetts who in the aggregate handled about 75 per cent of the lobsters distributed in the United States. It was a fine idea, and undertook to promote most of the marketing ideas described here. Most of all, it was a uniting of dealers to accomplish improvements which one firm alone could not do. Unfortunately, it has gone out of existence because there was not enough belief in its benefits, and consequently not enough financial support.

Dealers are often as sot and fiercely independent as lobstermen. They go to dealers' meetings not to cooperate as much as to make sure that no one else is making any more money than they are. This lack of cooperative spirit has broken up cooperative after cooperative. Yet they keep forming. Why? Because, perhaps, underneath this independence is the half-awake instinct that only through some sacrifice of individuality can a greater good be achieved. Some day either some cooperative of dealers is going to work voluntarily or successful fishermen cooperatives are going to force them to work.

The solution of most of the lobster marketing problems lies in the education of all parties involved. Each state should be able to help in showing the way.

X

Research

A small-scale federal lobster investigation began in 1939 at Boothbay Harbor, Maine. The principal objective was to study ways of increasing the production of fourth-stage lobsters in the lobster-rearing station operated by the Maine Department of Sea and Shore Fisheries in cooperation with the U. S. Bureau of Fisheries.[1] The scope of the investigation was expanded to study certain biological aspects, i.e., lobster migrations, early life history, growth distribution and habits of the sub-legal sizes, and size composition of the catches. During World War II, the work was curtailed as personnel devoted most of their efforts to wartime duties. In 1947, the federal lobster investigation was ended. At that time the two principal lobster-producing states—Maine and Massachusetts—had begun their own lobster studies. Because lobster research appeared to be more of a state than a federal matter, the Fish and Wildlife Service was pleased to have the states assume the responsibility.

At this time (1960), lobster research is carried on by Maine and Massachusetts, but only on a limited scale. Maine's efforts have been principally directed towards assisting the industry with some of the practical problems such as testing new types of lobster traps, devising better methods of holding live lobsters in recirculated water, disinfecting lobster pounds, and providing trouble-shooting services to operators of tank storage facilities, as well as some basic biological research. These activities are carried on intermittently by biologists engaged primarily in other studies. A Saltonstall-Kennedy grant to the Maine Department of Sea and Shore Fisheries has financed an economic-biological study of the lobster industry.

In Massachusetts, lobster research is now confined principally to biological observations on the age, growth, and

[1] Pages 149-50 are quoted from Leslie W. Scattergood and Robert L. Dow, " The Lobster Industry."

feeding habits of lobsters at the lobster-rearing station in Martha's Vineyard.

There are a number of significant problems which should be studied. They are:

1. The factors that affect abundance and productivity (populations dynamics)

2. Improvements in handling, holding, and shipping live lobsters

3. Product diversification

4. The economic-biological management of the resource.

The estimated cost of these studies is $230,000.

In addition, in its 20th Biennial Report, the Department of Sea and Shore Fisheries lists three more specific problems:

1. A study of the life history of the American lobster (Homarus americanus). We believe that this study would be most valuable and should provide much information on sound conservation and marketing practices.

2. An evaluation of predation (living by prey) as a factor affecting the abundance of lobsters. Both producers and lobster dealers should benefit from this study, and the information gathered should be of great use in any further work on processing and marketing.

3. Investigation of natural and synthetic lobster baits. In an off year, bait could become the number one problem of the Maine lobster fishing industry. As it is, it constitutes the greatest single expense to the producer. For the past two years there has been an abundance of herring which has prevented the situation from becoming critical. But if the groundfish and redfish industry should decline and if there should be a year when herring are scarce, lobster fishermen could be faced with their most serious problem to date. For these reasons, we feel that these bait studies are of the greatest importance.[2]

---

[2] *See* pages 74-83.

A Plea for Research. An editorial in *Maine Coast Fisherman,* January, 1950, is worth repeating here:

"Those darned fools at the Boothbay Laboratory don't amount to a damn."

Well, it looks like you're right; they haven't found the cure for pink tail, and they haven't helped much to make lobsters breed faster.

So what's the use of keeping on with them? Why not close down the whole Lobster Rearing Station and save money?

Maybe we might be helped in deciding if we look backwards a couple of generations to a man named Pasteur—the man who discovered the pasteurization of milk. He was a scientist and a biologist like the men who run the Boothbay Lab. He set out to learn what bacteria did to wine and other things, including milk. It took him ten years of patient plugging—and getting jeered at most of the time—to discover how to treat milk to make it safe. Of course, today his name is honored and lots of babies owe their lives to him. But Pasteur wasn't any hero during those weary years of trying, test by test, to learn the answer.

The staff at Boothbay is good, and they're tackling our problems in the best ways known to science. But it takes time—a lot of it—and it takes a lot of patience to plug ahead when you don't get results right away; particularly if lobstermen keep hollering for more show for their money.

We ought to sit tight. The Boothbay scientists are learning more all the time. Along with the big searches, they are learning sidelines about lobsters. Frequently, Sea and Shore Fisheries comes out with a leaflet giving more knowledge about lobsters. It is real dope—not guesswork. How are you going to treat this information? Are you going to jeer, or are you going to think, "That crowd has found out by tests what is so and what isn't so. I'll bank on it that they are right."

Let's back them up. Quit kicking and start listening and believing.

Suggested Lines of Thought for Inventors

Thomas A. Edison said: " There is a way to do it better. Find it."

1. *Artificial bait.* Try phosphorus as a component of a bait. It is an important chemical to a lobster, so he must seek it.[3]

The fluids squeezed and dried out of fish scrap to make fishmeal should have all the components attractive to a lobster. A lobster senses his bait through water-borne attractants, and these fluids should have them. Yet it is an expense to the fishmeal people to get rid of the fluids.

So why not use them as a lure?

It should be much easier to learn how to dispense fish fluids than it is to discover the chemicals in brim (the scraps after filleting a fish) for which a lobster yearns. Remember that the chemicals in fish scrap change from hour to hour as the fish decays, and it might take a lifetime of chemical research to find what a lobster craves. It would not be easy to evolve a dispenser which releases such a lure, a drop at a time, but any invention which can be held in the hand and studied is very much easier to understand than the intangibles of a chemical action.

Such a bait probably would have to be heavily salted, (both to preserve it and to make it heavier than sea-water), and then carefully filtered.

Another suggestion:

Learn how to introduce *strong* trimethylamine (stronger than a 10 per cent solution) into sea water, and do it slowly, a bubble at a time. Its odor makes it difficult to handle, but it has shown evidence of being a lobster attractant. Perhaps Dr. Harry Lee can explain how he dispersed his gas.[4]

---

[3] *See* page 28.

[4] *See* page 83.

2. *Lights for lures.* Try lights *outside* of a pot, perhaps four or five feet above. All experiments with lights have been made with the light inside the pot. Inside, a light might repel a lobster from entering. A light outside might lure a lobster into the neighborhood of the pot without scaring him from entering. The attraction of the bait might complete his capture.

Devise a practical way to shake up a neon-and-mercury glass bulb so that it will light up. It has shown some promise as a lure.[5]

3. *Brands.* Develop an inexpensive and quick way of marking a lobster.[6]

4. *Better lobster pots.* Design a better lobster pot, or even only part of a pot. It is reported that the base of a pot made of plastic is being developed in Boothbay.

a. Get away from wood and its buoyancy and its attraction to borers
b. Make it collapsible
c. Improve its shape[7]
d. Perhaps make it smaller by eliminating the parlor and use instead some other trapping device, such as the " inhibitor " in the Leakey pot. *He* says it works.[8]

5. *Research in anti-biotics.* Work further with anti-biotics.[9] If an unscaled and ungutted fish can have its flesh penetrated and preserved, then there should be a way to impregnate a lobster with the chemical. And the lobster is alive to circulate the chemical throughout his bloodstream—a benefit the dead fish did not have.

6. *A slogan.* Devise a good slogan saying that " two chicken lobsters are a tastier meal than one large lobster."

7. *Other uses.* Find out how to use the carapace (the hard-shelled part of the lobster).

---

[5] *Ibid.*
[6] *See* pages 142-44.
[7] *See* page 44.
[8] *See* page 49.
[9] *See* pages 124-25.

XI

Cooking and Preparing

Lobsters are eaten boiled, broiled alive, baked-stuffed, and in numerous dishes such as lobster Newburg, where the meat is not served in the shell. Boiled lobster either hot or cold is by far the most common method, and the easiest for the cook.

Actually, the preferred method of cooking is not boiling, but steaming. The lobster is placed in about one inch of boiling water to which a heaping teaspoonful of salt has been added. Fully immersing a lobster in boiling water will cook out some of its flavor—just as boiling a fowl will cook out the chicken broth. For a small lobster fifteen minutes' steaming will suffice. For larger lobsters, from twenty to thirty minutes, if the water is really boiling when the lobster is put in the pot. Do not remove the plugs or bands until *after* the lobster is cooked.

Some cooks claim that they seal in the flavor of a cooked lobster if they immerse it in cold water immediately after cooking. Whether or not this is so, the cooling off makes the handling of him much easier.

Getting the meat out of the shell is the trick of the whole serving, and can seem to be too great a feat if the housewife has not seen it done. It is not too difficult. Put a large bowl in your sink and work over that so that you will catch some of the juice as you break open the lobster (it makes a wonderful bisque, when combined with milk and butter and seasonings to taste).

1. Break the lobster apart where the jointed tail section joins the solid part of the shell. Grab one part in each fist and twist. It is easy, and the whole lobster will come apart, retaining its meat in each section.

2. Push the meat out of the tail section. This is best done by breaking off the five little fins at the extreme tail of the lobster. The end tip of inner meat is

thereby exposed, and the whole meat in the tail can be pushed forward and out of the shell by pressure of the thumb. Another way is to split the underneath length of the tail section with a carving knife and break the shell apart. Use a stiff knife.

3. Slice this tail meat down its length. You are looking for the lower intestine, to pick out and remove it. It is the only part of the innards of a lobster that is not edible. In a freshly caught lobster, this intestine looks like a couple of inches of black string. The black material is dung, and if the color is present it shows that the lobster has not emptied the bowel, as it will do if kept a few days in a tank. It is one of the best tests of the freshness of your lobster. An emptied bowel does not mean your lobster is not good, healthy and vigorous when cooked, but only that he is not so fresh out of the sea.

4. Break off both arms where they attach to the body
Remove the plugs or bands
Break the claws away from the arms
Break the two parts of the claws apart

5. Break the shell of claws and arms with a hammer or nut cracker. Break only enough to enable the diner to pick out the meat. Do not excessively crush the inner meat. (Lobster shears are buyable and make all these cuttings or crushing operations much easier.)

6. Cut down the length of the solid-shelled part of the lobster. Cut on a line between where the walking legs join the body. With one fist on each side of the body break the shell apart. You have exposed the upper cavity of the body. The greenish material is tomalley or liver, and is choice, in taste if not in appearance. It is often used for *hors d'oeuvres.* The salmon colored material is known as " coral " and is unlaid eggs, also edible but of less taste. Break off the walking legs and suck out the meat.

Serve the lobster with melted butter into which each mouthful should be dipped. Provide nut-picks for easy removal of the meat.

Note: The jointed tail of a lobster should always curl up on itself whether the lobster is supposedly alive or cooked. You should be able to uncurl this tail with your hand, and have it snap back to the curled position. If this does not happen in a " live " lobster, then that lobster is dead or dying. If it does not snap back in a boiled lobster, then the lobster was dead before he was boiled. Most restaurants know this and will take back without fuss a lobster in this condition.

XII

So You Want to be a Lobsterman?

Against:

This chapter is primarily concerned with the lobster fisherman but dwells on the other sides of the lobster industry such as the lobster buyer, the business of pounding lobsters, and the wholesaler.

It is natural that any boy (or girl for that matter, and there are several successful lobsterwomen) who lives near the sea may turn to lobstering for his lifework. But it is a different sort of life than most people experience. It can be a good life and a profitable one: **IF**

If you can stand its loneliness.

A lobsterman is up before dawn and is usually alone during his fishing. It is surprising how few lobsterboats are equipped with radios whose music would ease the monotony, as they do in factories.

Sure, some fishermen who have a large number of traps (perhaps up to 500) have company and take along a helper if they plan to haul half of the string every day. But this is overhead expense and can be the bane of a lobsterman as it is in any other industry. It divides the profit though the increased catch may make up for the loss.

The man whose interests are centered on things outside himself (the extrovert) may be less happy in a lobsterman's loneliness than will the man who finds his satisfaction with his own inner thoughts (the introvert). But there is no such thing as being wholly introvert or wholly extrovert. All of us have some of each characteristic. However, once a lobsterman has reached his fishing grounds he is busy and has little time for daydreaming.

Can you do without company while you are working?

---

* reprinted courtesy of National Fisherman

If you will realize that it is a poorly paid profession. Or more exactly, it is poorly paid for the majority who could probably earn a better day's pay working for Bath Iron Works. But this shipyard is not nearby for most men nor does such supervised and confining work appeal to men who have an independent streak – they have got to feel free and be their own boss.

There are over 5,000 registered lobstermen in Maine alone, and they catch approximately 20,000,000 pounds of lobsters in an average year. That averages out to 4,000 pounds of lobsters per man. It includes the little man with only 20 pots fishing from a dory as well as the expert who catches more than average.

Yet, 4,000 pounds per man in a year, at the recent average price of 75 cents per pound, only comes to $3,000 per year, and out of this must come the cost of bait, gasoline, and gear maintenance (30 per cent loss of pots per season is not uncommon).

You must be *determined* to be a top-liner if you want to earn a good living as a lobsterman. Education is the probable answer.

Lobstering does not have to be poorly paid, and isn't, for a few top-liners. It isn't easy to discover what makes one lobsterman much more successful than another, any more than you can put your finger on one doctor's success versus another doctor's lack of it. Probably it's the knowledge of his art (skill) that is an outstanding requisite.

Notice that hard work is not listed here, because most lobstermen are hard workers. Good luck seems to be of small influence, since a bad storm and lost gear can hurt the expert lobsterman as badly as the dub, though perhaps the expert will read the signs of an approaching gale and get some of his pots ashore.

If knowledge is the key to becoming an outstanding fisherman then what must this man know, and how can he acquire the education?

In the first place, the young fisherman must *want* to

know more about lobsters. If he isn't smarter than lobsters in learning their habits and their appetites then he will not become a top-liner. It sounds easy, doesn't it? But it is not.

There are countless lobstermen who have fished all their lives who rarely question the effectiveness of their gear or will listen to suggestions, and are much ruffled at the idea that anyone outside their trade can tell them anything.

It is education that is lacking (not book-learning education but education in their trade), and it is pretty hard to teach an old dog new tricks.

Education can start by apprenticing yourself to an experienced lobsterman for a season. He should be a successful fisherman, but above all he should be a man who will share his knowledge, i.e., how does he know that it is good fishing ground off Jones's Point in August but not in June, and why is he changing bait from redfish to herring? And if he is a top-liner, notice how poorer lobstermen drop their pots around his set, and how they fumble around to find his new fishing grounds when he moves – always following, not leading.

If you set your heart on being more than an average lobsterman, are you prepared to learn, and keep on learning *from any source,* even the summer visitor (who may be a distinguished developer of new ideas) who innocently asks, "Why don't you start lobstering later in the morning instead of at the crack of dawn?"

Most lobstermen wouldn't bother to answer this question, and would glare at the questioner in stony-eyed contempt. But a man who is continually searching for education will think, "That's a thought. Are our reasons good enough today?"

It is unfortunate that the solitariness of a lobsterman's life, and the rareness of his contacts with people outside his own small community very definitely limit his knowledge of what other men are doing. It must, and it does, result in narrowmindedness. You laugh if a neighbor says, "My father lobstered for fifty years. He knew where the ledges and feeding grounds were. What was good enough for him is good enough for me."

Yet, will you turn up your nose at equipping with a depth recorder, calling it new fangled, unnecessary and sissy fishing gear? The ledges don't shift but your memory may. Or will you try out a new pot design if it is offered you?

Education is probably the greatest need for the whole lobster industry. Very few lobstermen will recognize this. They are so close to their job and so steeped in their habits that they can't or won't draw off and size up the whole picture.

Are you ready and capable of doing this? It is one of the abilities of the top-liner to see his weaknesses – that is the first step toward correcting them.

You may doubt the statement that many lobstermen are close-minded, but consider today's lobster pot. It hasn't changed in over 100 years except for the addition of the parlor. How many other tools haven't been improved in 100 years, except the lobster pot?

Even the frying pan is less clumsy and less greasy and the hoe is of better steel and lighter. Have the number of men required to catch 1,000 pounds of lobsters been appreciably reduced?

Pots are still made of wood, and become lighter when immersed in sea water when they should become heavier to anchor them to the sea floor. They still will allow trapped lobsters to escape. They still can be rolled about the ocean floor in a storm, and smashed. They still are being chewed up by toredo. Is this advancement?

Advancement of lobstering practices will have to come from today's apprentices, at least from those who see the need for educating themselves, and will seek the education.

Openmindedness is the opposite of narrowmindedness. Will you *try anything* which promises to benefit your trade? Lots of fishermen won't be bothered.

It has been said, "The very first essential of any real

education is to observe concrete facts. Unless you do this you have no material out of which to manufacture knowledge. Compare the facts you have observed; and you will find yourself thinking out conclusions. These conclusions are real knowledge, and they are your own."

Education includes testing the truth of many accepted practices, and weeding out " old wives tales." Some lobstermen insist on using dyed-green nylon twine for their pot heads. Others insist that only brown or white are effective. Do you believe there is any difference? There may be, but no scientific tests have been published to prove the point. Or are these beliefs just " sotness "?

On the other hand, there are many beliefs of lobstermen which are true and which have been proven over years of use, but it is surprising the number of practices that are effective but to which the lobstermen attribute the wrong reasons.

A new oak trap won't fish until it has been soaked for a week in sea water to make it " water-logged." Of course, it will soak up water in a week, but it is more likely that it is the acid leaching out of the oak which makes it fishable.

To be sure, the brash young beginner has to learn that there are " know-hows " of the old-timers which can't be overlooked. For example, the young engineer fresh out of college has learned to accurately measure the heat of a flame with a pyrometer (a heat thermometer). Then he sees the village blacksmith haul a white-hot piece of iron out of his fire, hold it up to squint at it, and declare, " That's just about hot enough." The young engineer is aghast at such slipshod methods of judging heat.

But as he grows older and more experienced he is surprised to learn how accurate is the blacksmith's judgment. Years of experience with glowing iron have given him a knowledge beyond the understanding of the untaught. An old-time lobsterman has learned similar valuable ways of judging.

There are several college graduates who are lobstermen,

and they are highly successful. In talking with them one is impressed that their success is in no way due to their "book-learning" but in the training of their minds to question the accepted means and gear for fishing, and their willingness to study the lobster and outsmart him.

If you can stand the rugged life.

Lobstering is a rugged life. The summer visitor sees a lobsterman hauling his pots on a warm summer day with little wind and no sea running. It looks to be an ideal way of earning a living.

But let this same visitor get up before dawn, lug aboard three bushels of stinking fish bait with five gallons of gas and row them out to his vessel. It may be raining and blowing smart. The sea will be rough, and it will be penetratingly cold.

As soon as he has passed the lee of the harbor the visitor will be seasick and oh, so miserable, and glad to take shelter in the cuddy. The lobsterman may not be seasick but he can be miserable too, and he's got to continue most of the day, and darned glad to creep home to a quiet harbor.

Multiply these miseries for fishing in the colder weather of early spring and late fall, and you test a lobsterman's ruggedness.

Then consider the man who fishes all winter. He probably doesn't put out oftener than every other day but that is no job for a weakling. Can your hands stand being continuously wet with 40° water even though you wear cotton gloves? Yet it pays, for the scarcity of lobsters in winter nearly doubles the price for your catch.

If you have the heart to meet discouragement.

Imagine it, all day out in the cold and only 10 lobsters to show for it – not enough to pay for your gas. You shift the location of your pots, you change your bait, and still no decent catch all week – the lobsters just aren't feeding.

Then you run into a three-day nor'easter when you can't go out. After the sea calms down you spend two days just hunting for lost pots (at $3 a pot). Some of them will be lost for good, having been rolled over and over by the waves thus winding the warps around the body of the traps and drawing the buoys down out of sight. Others will have been shifted by the waves and you zigzag back and forth over the sea searching for them. You will wearily put for home with a deckload of smashed pots to be repaired when you are next stormbound. Up to 30 per cent of a man's pots are lost each year.

Is your courage strong enough to stand this and look beyond to see that it is the *average* results that count, not just a few days of hard luck?

Or take the period of good weather when lobsters are plentiful and your catch is good. It is very heartening — until you sell your catch, and find the price is 15 cents a pound less than it was yesterday — for there is a glut of lobsters.

Maybe you say, "This is a hell of a business," or maybe you get mad at your buyer and shift to another buyer who offers a quarter cent more per pound.

The top-liner will rarely do either of these things. *He* knows that supply governs demand (and prices) and the dealer shouldn't be blamed. He also knows it doesn't pay to get mad with his buyer, for the lobsterman who isn't loyal to his buyer won't find the buyer loyal to him and willing to take his catch when the buyer is already loaded up.

It is hard to imagine greater narrowmindedness than that of a fisherman who has been buying gear from his buyer on credit all winter, yet who shifts from this buyer during the catching season because someone else offers him a quarter of a cent more. It happens.

If your home port is a good enough location.

If you live on a harbor which supports 200 lobstermen but only two buyers, you are in the hands of those buyers and they can be as arrogant as they please. But if there are more buyers, you can pick the one who treats you best *year in and year out.*

Of course, it may be necessary to switch buyers but the top-liner does this infrequently. A man who has a record of often changing jobs is a poor bet for any employer, and so is the lobsterman who changes his agent often.

It is not easy to pull up stakes and move to another port, but it is better to start under the best conditions, for once you have learned your fishing grounds it will be a hard job to locate the best reefs, etc., out from another port.

Another consideration is the number of lobstermen fishing out of your port. There are too many lobstermen in Maine as it is; there are so many that only a few can earn a decent living. And there are only so many lobsters to be caught.

So if there are two lobstermen for each lobster caught, there is little profit in fishing out of your home port. Educate yourself on what harbors are most promising. The Department of Sea and Shore Fisheries can help you (not just the wardens, they know only one section of the coast), if you write to Augusta.

Two other facts to investigate: Can spare parts for your motor be procured nearby? Is there a dependable source of bait?

For:

You have heard the " outs " of becoming a lobsterman, now consider the advantages.

It is a life of independence.

This is very important to many a man, and perhaps more so than usual to Maine men. Your pioneer stock had to stand alone and the trait has not been bred out. It seems to be common to many men in small coast towns to rebel against working for a boss; they are not happy in supervised or confining work, and no man does his best if he is not happy in his work.

If this independence is a strong part of your nature and you live by the sea, there isn't much choice in what work will suit you best.

Oh sure, you can buy a truck and set up an independent express business of your own, but you are competing against large concerns and there is the uncertainty of maintaining profitable runs. One breakdown tying you up for several days and you have lost a customer, maybe your big one. Not so with lobstering. You can be laid up with a broken leg and still get back into business as soon as you are well.

It is a rewarding life.

If you educate yourself to be a top-liner. A few *really good* lobstermen clear up to $10,000 a year, and that is wealth in a small coast town.

There are other rewards too. Maine folk are kindly, and you will live among them and among people who share your interests. You will enjoy the winter work in your shop, building pots, with perhaps some of your cronies or retired lobstermen sitting around the stove, smoking and yarning.

You will have the satisfaction of actually *seeing* how much you have accomplished in each day's haul. Compare this with a salesman who doesn't get an order on the same day that he makes his best selling approach. *His* results are often in the future when the glow of achievement is gone.

It is a healthy life.

Lobstermen dress to meet the weather, and being outdoors all day is the healthiest sort of life.

It seems to be a safe life, for few lobstermen are lost at sea. There is a brotherly feeling among them and if one man hasn't shown up at night the whole fleet of home boats will put out and search all night for his broken-down vessel. Few lobstermen are lost overboard though they are usually alone and are sometimes careless in how they fling the warp over the deck when hauling a pot. It is surprising that the boatman doesn't get his foot caught in a loop of the warp when the pot is dumped overside. It is probable that accidents in driving a truck or being run down in a city street are more common than comparative mishaps in lobstering.

It is an interesting job.

The interest lies in the repeated anticipation of what the

catch will be in the next pot you haul; and, if it is empty, hope and interest are revived for the succeeding haul.

It is a satisfaction to prove that you have judged correctly where the lobsters will be thick, and to know *exactly* where Fireman's Ledge is located, and recall that it is an area which hasn't been fished by anyone in over a month – it used to be fine fishing grounds until everyone learned of it and fished it out.

It is a satisfaction to prove your sense of direction and to find your next string of pots in a dense fog. It pleases you to see that Harry Jones has dropped his pots 200 yards too far to the east of Jenkins Ledge. *You* know exactly where it is because you took cross bearings on its position and wrote them down (one top-liner has done this for every good fishing spot in his area) and you'll chuckle tomorrow when you see Harry Jones has moved his pots up alongside of yours – after you've caught the cream of the lobsters.

The art of being a top-liner can be passed along.

To your son, for instance, and it might be a more valuable inheritance than your real estate, that is, if he is ready to learn and you spur him on to be a better fisherman than even you are. It is a great satisfaction to see your boy bring in better catches than you do – because he *knows* more about lobsters than you.

He can learn not only from you, but from publications of the Maine Department of Sea and Shore Fisheries and from books.

Further Steps:

Do you want to advance to become a buyer?

It is the next step above being a lobsterman. But the job has problems and requires you to have an education.

In the first place you would need capital:

1. To pay cash for the lobsters.
2. To buy bait.
3. To furnish credit to lobstermen when they are outfitting.

4. To carry the tanked lobsters over a slump in the market.

This sounds easy – but buying and selling lobsters is a risky business. Education for a buyer is much more expensive than it is for a fisherman. Note the number of new buyers who go out of business after one or two seasons.

You won't acquire overnight the judgment on how much to pay your fishermen, or whether to unload your stock of lobsters in anticipation of a falling market, or which lobsterman you can safely give credit to. Will you want to go it alone or will you be smart enough to see the advantages of joining with other dealers in a sort of union to overcome the small jealousies that continually crop up?

The present-day dealers had to start small and learn through mistakes. You can too if your mistakes are not too costly.

Do you want to take the next step and operate a pound?

This is the biggest risk of all, but it is the operation which can bring in the real money. It takes the most capital too – buying the pound – and stocking it with many thousands of pounds of lobsters, and holding them for the high prices of winter. It sounds as though only capital were necessary to make pounding a success. But the risks are there and they are the biggest risks of all.

A few seasons ago a pound owner of two generations of experience lost all his lobsters (20,000 pounds), and even Sea and Shore Fisheries experts aren't sure why. In another and smaller pound all the lobsters died because of an influx of fresh water from spring freshets. And there is always the threat of red-tail disease.

On the other hand, there seem to be fewer failures among pound operators than in other branches of lobstering. Perhaps they know more.

It is certainly reasonable that if you buy soft-shelled lobsters at a reduced price and lighter weight, and can hold them until they harden up and flesh out, you can make a handsome profit when the price goes way up (as it does in winter). Many pounds stock up and unload several times a year.

Would you want to step into wholesaling?

This branch of lobstering is somewhat different from the previously discussed branches of the industry. It requires a profound knowledge of the market, for it is the wholesaler who determines the prices paid all down the line, even to the fisherman. And it requires a clientele of customers.

One firm in Rockland was started by a man whose main asset was a list of New York customers to whom he had previously sold on commission. His market was all set up and waiting before he commenced wholesale buying.

To sum up:

The lobster industry is big business.

It can be a good career for you if you will educate yourself and aim high.

You can go as far as your abilities and knowledge will permit.

BIBLIOGRAPHY

Baird, Frederick T., Jr., "Lobster Plugs and Their Effect on the Meat of the Lobster's Claw." S&SF*: Research Bulletin #2 (March, 1950).

Barnes, Ernest W., Bulletin (House No. 2051). Massachusetts Division of Fisheries and Game.

Bramsnaes, F., and Boetius, Jan, "Storage of Live Lobsters." Physiological Laboratory, Charlottenlund, Denmark.

Dow, Robert L. "The Story of the Maine Lobster." S&SF (Revised 1950; out of print).

——— "The Role of Traps in the Maine Lobster Industry." Part of Fisheries Education Series Unit No. 7 on "The Maine Lobster" (July, 1958).

——— and Baird, Frederick T., Jr., "Methods to Reduce Borer Damage to Lobster Traps." S&SF: Technical Bulletin #3 (1953).

Harriman, Donald M.; and Scattergood, Leslie W., "The Role of Holding Pounds in the Maine Lobster Industry." Washington, D. C.: *Commercial Fisheries Review* (XXI, 5) 1959.

——— "The American Lobster." Bulletin #74. Washington, D. C.: U. S. Fish and Wildlife Service.

Getchell, John S. "Study of Abnormal Shrinkage of Maine Lobsters ("Red Tail") with Observations and Recommendations. S&SF Bulletin (1949).

——— "Study of the Effect of Recirculated Natural and Artificial Sea Water on the Mortality of Lobsters." S&SF Research Bulletin #11 (1953).

——— and Highlands, Matthew, "Processing Lobster and Lobster Meat for Freezing and Storage." University of Maine, Orono: Bulletin #558 (1957).

Goggins, Philip L., "The Storage of Live Lobsters in Recirculated-Refrigerated Tanks." S&SF, 1960.

Goode, George Brown, *Fisheries and Fishery Industries of the United States.* Prepared through the cooperation of the Commissioner of Fisheries, and a Staff of Associates 1884-1887. U. S. Government Printing Office (1911).

Harriman, Donald, "The Gas Disease in Lobsters." Paper given before the Northeastern Section, American Fisheries Society. S&SF, 1955.

Herrick, Francis H., "The Natural History of the American Lobster." Bulletin of Fisheries, Vol. XXIX, 1909.

* Maine Department of Sea and Shore Fisheries.

Prudden, T. M. "Artificial Baits–LobLure." *Maine Coast Fisherman.*

——— "Lights for Lures." *Maine Coast Fisherman.*

Scattergood, Leslie W., and Dow, Robert L., "The Lobster Industry." Washington, D. C.: Bureau of Commercial Fisheries.

Schroeder, William C., "The Lobster, *Homarus americanus,* and the red crab, *Geryon quinquedens,* in the offshore waters of the western North Atlantic." Woods Hole Oceanographic Institution.

Taylor, Clyde, "Study of Lobster Shell Disease with Observations and Recommendations." S&SF Bulletin, 1949.

Thomas, H. J., "A Comparison of Some Methods Used in Lobster Fishing." Marine Laboratory, Aberdeen, Scotland.

——— "Lobster Storage," Marine Laboratory, Aberdeen.

——— "Practical Hints for Lobstermen." Marine Laboratory, Aberdeen.

——— "Lobster and Crab Fisheries in Scotland." Maine Laboratory, Aberdeen.

——— "The Efficiency of Fishing Methods Employed in the Capture of Lobsters and Crabs." International Council for the Exploration of the Sea, Charlottenlund, Denmark.

Wilder, D. G. "Lobster Migration." Fisheries Research Board of Canada *(Maine Coast Fisherman).*

"Acclimatization" (Note No. 137). Canada's Atlantic Biological Station.

"Plea for Research." *Maine Coast Fisherman.*

"New Ways to Keep Food Fresh." *The Saturday Evening Post.*

"Freeze-Drying." Courtesy *Time,* copyright Time, Inc. 1957.